CW01459374

# Introducing Health Care in Times Past

# OTHER BOOKS BY IAN WALLER

## Published by Family History Books
*Family History Research Challenges and How to Solve Them*
*Introducing Manorial Records*
*Introducing Nonconformist Records*

## Published by the Society of Genealogists
*My Ancestor was an Agricultural Labourer*
*My Ancestor was in the Royal Navy*
*My Ancestor was a Leather Worker*
*My Ancestor was a Mormon*

All titles are available from www.familyhistorybooksonline.com

**Introducing Health Care in Times Past**

# How our ancestors coped with illness and death

## Volume 2: Diseases, Remedies, Epidemics and Accidents

Ian H Waller FSG FGRA

Published by

Family History Books
the publishing imprint of the Family History Federation
a registered charity number 1038721


P.O. Box 62 Sheringham, Norfolk NR26 9AR


ISBN: 9781916599062


First published 2024


Copyright © Ian H Waller and Family History Books 2024


Family History Books is the trading name of the
Federation of Family History Societies (Services) Ltd

All rights reserved. No part of this book may be reproduced, or stored
in a retrieval system or transmitted in any form or by any means,
electronic, mechanical, photocopying, recording or otherwise, without
the prior approval of the Family History Federation.

Ian H Waller FSG FGRA has asserted his rights to be identified as the
author of his original work.

Typeset by Chapter One Book Design

Printed by Henry Ling Limited
The Dorset Press
Dorchester DT1 1HD

# IMPORTANT INFORMATION

The vast extent of the original text and its contents could not be contained successfully in one book alone. There is so much information within 172,000-odd words that the publishers, in agreement with the author, made the decision to present this comprehensive text as a series of four volumes under a single main title.

Each volume has a subtitle which clearly refers to its specific contents. The four volumes are:

Volume 1      Medical Practices, Professions and Pioneers
Volume 2      Diseases, Remedies, Epidemics and Accidents
Volume 3      Births, Deaths, Funerals and Mental Illness
Volume 4      Military Medical Care

**For the benefit of readers, an indication of what is covered in each volume is shown below.**

**Volume 1** describes how medicine evolved through the centuries. It discusses various medicinal practices by *wise women and witches* in medieval times through to *quacks*, *apothecaries* and then how health care became more prioritised and organised with trained doctors, nurses and others. There are chapters on different kinds of hospitals from almshouses and poor law infirmaries to the more modern hospitals of today. It also discusses some famous medical pioneers and developments in heath care from very basic medical equipment to vaccinations and penicillin.

**Volume 2** covers diseases through the centuries in some detail ranging from *evil spirits in the head* in medieval times, various epidemics and hereditary diseases to childhood disorders. The section on accidents at work covers agricultural work to the Industrial Revolution and much more. This volume also examines some unusual cures and remedies, especially those in earlier times, and uncovers some myths and folklore too.

**Volume 3** is all about birth, death and funerals. It covers how our ancestors dealt with childbirth centuries ago from basic care in medieval times to Victorian trends – and includes some odd superstitions about childbirth too. As sure as night follows day, death follows birth and the causes of death are examined in detail in this volume. This volume includes extensive details about funerals and how they have changed over the years. The volume ends by discussing the asylum system and how our ancestors dealt with mental illnesses.

**Volume 4** covers all aspects of medical care in the military from the Crusades in the twelfth century, the Battle of Agincourt, the Napoleonic and Crimean Wars through to the extensive care dealing with casualties in both world wars. The methods of transporting the wounded in the war zones are examined including the various military and volunteer groups that were involved such as naval nursing, volunteer aid detachments, the British Red Cross and many others. There are also extensive details of medicine, heath care and surgery at sea. This volume ends with the transition to the NHS and details about the Wellcome Institute for the History of Medicine.

# VOLUME 2

# Diseases, Remedies, Epidemics and Accidents

# ACKNOWLEDGMENTS

This series of books has been some years in the making with many weeks spent researching in archives and libraries including some specialist ones.

I wish to thank Family History Books who agreed to publish this extensive study. I couldn't have done it without the splendid editorial team and their facilitator, Jacqui Simkins, who steered everyone calmly through some tricky decisions.

No author can work without a good proofreader. I have been fortunate to work with Suzie Woodward for some years, and on this series she also did extensive work as copy editor. Her forensic eye for detail and all her helpful suggestions have been invaluable and I extend my warmest thanks and appreciation for all her hard work – and her patience!

Ian Waller,
2024

# CONTENTS

# TIMELINE

**The following timeline highlights some of the more significant events which took place through the centuries.**

| | |
|---|---|
| **12th cent.** | During the Crusades doctors began using Arabian medicine to treat wounds and disease |
| **1173** | The established infirmary of St Mary Overie was renamed St Thomas' Hospital, London |
| **1267** | Spectacles and magnifying glasses using convex lenses to correct vision were developed |
| **1348–9** | The Black Death sweeps through Britain |
| **1415** | Battle of Agincourt |
| **1489** | Leonardo da Vinci began anatomical sketching of the human body |
| **1540** | English barbers and surgeons united to form the Barber-Surgeons' Company |
| **1540** | Andreas Vesalius discovered that blood flows through the septum in the heart |
| **1543** | Vesalius published *De humani corporis fabrica* [On the fabric of the human body] |
| **1570s** | Ligatures to stop bleeding and also ointments for wounds developed |
| **1590** | The microscope was perfected |
| **1628** | William Harvey published his work demonstrating that blood circulates, pumped by the heart |
| **1630** | Amputations first performed as a treatment for gangrene |
| **1656** | Christopher Wren demonstrated intravenous injection providing the basis for blood transfusion |

| | |
|---|---|
| **1658** | Dutch naturalist, Jan Swammerdam, observed red blood cells under the microscope |
| **1660s** | Thomas Sydenham, a London physician, believed that diagnosis is best done by close observation of symptoms |
| **1665** | The plague returned to London |
| **1666** | The Great Fire of London |
| **1674** | Antonie van Leeuwenhoek, the Father of Microbiology described red blood cells |
| **1676** | An amateur naturalist discovered bacteria |
| **1701** | Giacomo Pylarini, an Italian physician, oversees the first smallpox inoculations |
| **1713** | First asylum was established in Norwich – known as Bethel Hospital |
| **1717** | Lady Mary Wortley Montagu introduced subcutaneous variolation against smallpox to Britain |
| **1721** | Guy's Hospital, London founded |
| **1729** | Royal Infirmary, Edinburgh founded |
| **1731** | The first recorded appendectomy performed by English surgeon William Cookesley |
| **1739** | Queen Charlotte's Maternity Hospital, London founded |
| **1739** | First edition published of Samuel Sharp's A Treatise on the Operations of Surgery |
| **1753** | Dr James Lind published A treatise of scurvy following his research in the navy |
| **1796** | Edward Jenner developed a vaccination using cowpox to treat smallpox |
| **1799** | Humphrey Davy discovered the anaesthetic attributes of nitrous oxide (laughing gas) |
| **1816** | The stethoscope was invented by René Laennec in Paris |
| **1818** | The first successful blood transfusion to treat post-partum haemorrhage took place |
| **1842** | Edwin Chadwick published his Report on the Sanitary Conditions of the Labouring Population of Great Britain |
| **1846** | First successful use of ether as an anaesthetic in surgery |
| **1847** | Prof. James Young Simpson demonstrated chloroform through an experiment on his friends |

| | |
|---|---|
| **1846–8** | Prevention of the transmission of disease by washing hands before surgery realised |
| **1853** | Hypodermic syringe invented independently by both Alexander Wood and Charles Pravaz |
| **1853** | The Vaccination Act made smallpox vaccination compulsory from 1 August |
| **1854** | Florence Nightingale and Betsi Cadwaladr improved care and hygiene in hospitals at Scutari |
| **1855** | Mary Seacole established the British Hotel for soldiers near Balaclava |
| **1858** | The Medical Act created the General Medical Council to regulate doctors' qualifications |
| **1861** | Louis Pasteur published his Germ Theory |
| **1865** | Elizabeth Garrett-Anderson became the first female doctor in Britain |
| **1867** | Joseph Lister began using carbolic acid to dress wounds to fight infection |
| **1870s** | Joseph Lister used carbolic acid spray during surgery |
| **1870s** | Together Robert Koch and Louis Pasteur established the germ theory of disease |
| **1876** | Robert Koch discovered the bacteria that causes anthrax |
| **1887** | First contact lenses were developed |
| **1890s** | Discovery of antitoxins, and development of vaccines for tetanus and diphtheria |
| **1893** | Isolation Hospitals Act enabling local authorities to establish hospitals for infectious diseases |
| **1895** | William Röntgen discovered X-rays |
| **1897** | Synthesized aspirin developed |
| **1898** | Marie Curie discovered the radioactive elements radium and polonium |
| **1901** | Blood types first classified into groups |
| **1906** | Frederick Gowland Hopkins suggested amino-acids are essential to health |
| **1907** | Education (Administrative Provisions) Act requires medical inspections in schools |
| **1908** | Old Age Pensions Act (pension commenced 1 January **1909**) |

| 1909 | Paul Ehrlich pioneers a cure for syphilis and introduces the process known as chemotherapy |
|------|---|
| 1911 | National Health Insurance Act became law (came into effect 1 July 1912) |
| 1913 | The electro-cardiograph (ECG) introduced for general use by Dr Paul Dudley White |
| 1914 | Marie Curie pioneered mobile X-ray facilities on the battlefields of the First World War |
| 1917 | Harold Gillies pioneered plastic surgery techniques to repair the faces of injured soldiers |
| 1918 | Discovery that trench fever was transmitted by lice |
| 1922 | Injected insulin used to treat diabetes for the first time |
| 1928 | First true antibiotic, penicillin, discovered by Alexander Fleming |
| 1947 | First successful defibrillation performed by Claude Black |
| 1948 | Start of the National Health Service in Britain |

# INTRODUCTION

Viewed from a modern perspective, it is difficult to believe that some treatments and remedies in years gone by were actually beneficial to the health of our ancestors. Many of those early cures were based on folklore, traditions handed down through generations and spiritual guidance; practitioners at that time had very limited medical knowledge so may not have known any different. In this second volume, we delve into almost every disease under the sun from medieval times onwards and then we examine the treatments and cures that were used – and there were some rather strange ones to be sure. Accidents at work were more common in earlier years and we explore why they happened and how they were treated. Finally, we scrutinise hereditary diseases and epidemics which affected the whole country.

# CHAPTER 1

# COMMON DISEASES AND REMEDIES
## 1600–1837

**Medieval diseases**

In medieval times no one knew how diseases were spread other than the fact that they were frequently widespread in both villages and towns. Physicians were considered to be skilled but their work was based on little knowledge of human anatomy. Experiments on dead bodies were strictly forbidden and physicians charged for their services which only the rich could afford. Many of their cures were bizarre and haphazard but some did have a sort of logic to them. Many physicians also had their own ideas about the causes of diseases, but at the time these were unproven. When a patient recovered, it was considered a sign that their diagnosed cure had worked; so it was repeated in other cases. If the cure did not work on another patient, then this was deemed the fault of the patient not of the diagnosed cure!

**Medieval cures**

Some of the early remedies are still in existence today in the form of alternative medicine and clearly were an aid to healing in times past. However, many are now obsolete and may even be considered bizarre. There are few records detailing their success or failure. It isn't until we reach the eighteenth and nineteenth century that we see significant advances in treatment.

People were encouraged to exercise their faith and take a pilgrimage to a holy shrine to show their love of God and this would cure them of illnesses, especially if they partook of holy water at the place of pilgrimage. Holy shrines and miracle healers were very meaningful to many generations of our ancestors; they were most important during in the Middle Ages when they were considered essential because secular medical treatment was extremely ineffective.

For centuries men have sought healing in the waters of natural springs because they were thought to be indispensable for cleansing and possessed of therapeutic powers. In medieval times people really believed that taking the waters would heal them.

In 1170 after the murder of Thomas à Becket, then Archbishop of Canterbury, people began dipping their fingers into his blood to receive the blessing from the martyr which resulted in claims of miracle healing. His blood was supposed to cure blindness, insanity, leprosy, and deafness. Within ten years of Becket's death, some 700 cases of healing supposedly happened in Canterbury.

Our ancestors were indoctrinated with the belief that keeping the four humours in a state of equilibrium was key to good health and that bloodletting was the most effective way to overcome any imbalance.

Bloodletting was done to balance the body fluids and when associated with astrology, if anyone was suffering from a fever, the bloodletting had to be done as soon as the moon had passed through the middle of the sign of Gemini. Evil spirits abounded and if thought to be *in the head,* then more drastic surgical action was taken. Strange liquid mixtures were used for other cures; tobacco juice was said to destroy head lice and ale soaked with lice was said to cure jaundice.

Gout, deafness and baldness could all be treated using some peculiar mixtures such as worms, pig's marrow and herbs or fox grease and hare gall. More drastic measures like red-hot pokers were used to cauterize wounds. One of the most bizarre cures was hanging red curtains around the bed of a smallpox patient. As they say these days in utter amazement ... you couldn't make it up! But this is exactly what the medieval medics did to help people. A full list of these bizarre mixtures, liquids and animal parts can be seen at appendix 1.

Many of our medieval ancestors just did not have access to medical interventions. When the Black Death swept through the country, the medical profession was powerless to prevent its spread. In the medieval period around thirty-five per cent of all newborn children died during or shortly after childbirth. However, illness in the Middle Ages was not a death sentence because there was a philosophy that following a healthy lifestyle meant people would not fall ill in the first place. By 1315, sleep was also considered important to health and it was recommended that everyone should sleep for at least one quarter of the day and also go for a walk daily. When you think about it, the same advice is being given out today in the twenty-first century.

## Diseases and remedies in the eighteenth and nineteenth centuries

Throughout the eighteenth and nineteenth centuries, obviously the same diseases and ailments seen earlier were still present, but with more medical people in the population, knowledge was being gained and new diseases were not only being discovered and named but also being treated to some extent.

Little had been known before about diseases like epilepsy, venereal disease, or internal digestive issues. Of course they had all existed before, but no one had really put a name to them, described them or knew much about them really. There were more physicians and apothecaries in Georgian times and they had been learning all the time and improving their skills, passing them on to each generation. So the existence of different and new cures and treatments used in the eighteenth and nineteenth centuries revealed that great advances in medicines and health had taken place.

In earlier medieval times, people really believed that water from natural springs was therapeutic and healing. Now in the 1700s, baths were frequently used. It was believed to be advantageous to the skin as well as helping those with mental difficulties.

Just as medieval monks and wise women used preparations made from plants and herbs, new liquid mixtures were being found and used to cure ailments such as eye inflammations and digestive complaints; gargles were also invented to treat throat and mouth problems. In fact, liquid preparations, often referred to as tonics, were composed of infusions to which syrups, extracts, powders or salts were added. They were used as laxatives and cough expectorants and to cure others ailments such as convulsions, epilepsy, digestive issues, fevers, dropsy, inflammation and severe pain.

Other remedies were discovered such as poultices, powders, liniments and ointments, all of which were used to cure a variety of common illnesses and which gave some relief. A complete list of eighteenth- and nineteenth-century ailments and their cures can be seen at appendix 2.

## Medical chests

In this age of self-medication most Regency homes of standing would have had a medical chest so that they could treat themselves for many minor ailments rather than call upon the services of an apothecary or a physician. Many of the treatments used then would have been superseded or banned today because they would be considered dangerous to health, but during Regency times they would have been acceptable medicines. Some items continued to be used throughout the Victorian era.

These are some of the really dangerous medications that were then in daily use:

- mercury with chalk as a purgative commonly referred to as *grey powder*
- red mercury oxide which was used as an antiseptic for a variety of lesions and in eye ointments
- laudanum used as an analgesic for pain relief
- chloroform for cough mixtures
- camphorated opium used in cough mixtures
- sulphuric acid diluted with quinine, brandy and orange essence to treat fevers.

Some medications not considered to be dangerous may still be found in medicine chests of today:

- tar used in ointments
- lavender oil in alcohol used for depression sickness
- zinc sulphate used as an astringent lotion
- rhubarb powder which is another laxative
- ammonia and oil for constipation and as a liniment often combined with almond oil
- camphor for flu, cholera or feverish colds
- *Epsom Salts* used as antacids (and good for tomato plants too!)
- peppermint to combat flatulence
- Milk of Magnesia used as an antacid and mild laxative
- cloves to give relief from toothache
- castor oil used as a laxative
- sherry drunk as an expectorant.

Many people also had a selection of patent or quack medicines in their home medicine cabinets. These quack medicines claimed to cure all the common illnesses. They were advertised in newspapers but local apothecaries and various outlets including postal service houses also sold them. During the later nineteenth century, the medical profession in conjunction with, and support of, the temperance organisations, crushed much of the trade because many of the medicines contained high levels of alcohol.

## Problems caused by Georgian vanities

Just for a moment, think back to those films you have might seen depicting these times. The best example is *The Madness of King George*. Picture the scenes which include groups of courtiers and in your mind's eye, you will probably see men with those ridiculous-looking high hairdos. Well, that was not their own hair because flamboyant wigs were in vogue in the latter part of the eighteenth century and mostly worn by men.

Both men and women achieved the fashionable pale hair colour by applying hair powder made from flour or starch which was puffed onto the head with a pair of bellows. For the Georgian 'big haired' look, the wealthy actually employed stylists who created elaborate wooden-framed structures often padded with horse hair. Curling tongs were developed to allow the hair to be wrapped around them and held in place until the curl had set. People also used a type of clay roller, heated in an oven and then applied that to the hair or wig. Heads would also be decorated with wax fruit, flowers or other outlandish adornments allowing hairstyles to stay in place for days at a time.

But these elaborate efforts in hair vanity caused problems too.

NOW Sᴿ YOU'R A COMPLEAT MACARONI.

*A fashionable man takes his hat off while strolling and his hairdresser assists him by supporting the weight of his large wig*

### Lice and the hair powder tax

It was quite common for the wearers of these ornate hairdos and wigs to become infested with lice, but in order that the hairstyle was not disturbed, handheld rods were available that could slide between the layers of hair so that the wearer could scratch the lice bites. If the lice bites became really itchy, they were treated with mercury which could and often did result in madness or even death. Some historians believe that the poisons contained in lice hair powders could have been a factor in how King George III became insane.

In May 1795 the government introduced the Duty on Hair Powder Act which levied a tax on the use of hair powder. Like all taxes it had a purpose and this tax was used to finance the wars with France in the late 1700s and early 1800s. The Act was not repealed until 1869.

The Act required everyone wishing to use hair powder to visit a stamp office to register and pay for an annual certificate costing one guinea (£1.1s.0d). There were certain exemptions including the Royal Family and their servants; clergymen with an income of under £100 a year and members of the armed forces. A father with more than two unmarried daughters could buy just two certificates that were valid for any number of daughters provided he notified the stamp office of the number. A householder could buy one certificate covering a number of servants. Ultimately, the use of hair powder dramatically declined because of the tax. In 1795 the tax raised £200,000 but by 1812 the amount raised was half that. In 1855 only 997 people paid the tax, most of them being servants. By 1869 the tax only yielded an annual revenue of £1,000.

Where they have survived, lists of certificates issued are likely to be found in local record offices. Some estate records provide information on the liveried servants who would likely have used hair powder.

### Teeth and tooth powders

Another aspect of Georgian vanity was the need to have pure white teeth. Upper-class Georgians indulged in all manner of sugary treats so their teeth were far from perfect. Tooth powders, made from cuttlefish bone and bicarbonate of soda, known commonly as spirit of vitriol (a form of sulphuric acid), were used to whiten teeth but this remedy had its faults as it tended to remove rather than protected the enamel on the teeth. This meant that many Georgians needed dental surgery.

In the eighteenth century, most dental surgery was undertaken without anaesthetic. Once the damaged teeth had been removed, new "live" teeth, purchased from a donor, were threaded directly into the sockets where the old teeth had been. Live teeth were often extracted from newly-deceased corpses so they may have introduced disease or infection into the mouth of the recipient. For those who could not afford a live tooth, there were alternatives which were crudely made from materials such as porcelain or ivory.

# CHAPTER 2

# EPIDEMICS

An epidemic is the rapid spread of a disease in a short period of time; epidemics usually last a long time within a population. The difference between an **epidemic** and a **pandemic** has nothing to do with how severe the disease is; it is the degree to which it has spread. An **epidemic** can be termed as regional whereas a **pandemic** cuts across international boundaries and are considered worldwide. Interestingly, Wikipedia has a page showing a list of all epidemics and pandemics; the list appears to be in order of the number of deaths caused. First on the list is Spanish flu which happened between 1918 and 1920 caused the most deaths as it was a worldwide pandemic.

Not all events which caused huge numbers of death were caused initially by diseases *per se*. The Great Famine of 1315–1317 caused many deaths in England. The people literally starved to death. This was a time when the country was predominantly populated by a rural and agricultural society. Records show that the weather in the early 1300s was particularly bad; this led to poor harvests so there was less food available to feed the population – a population which in fact was expanding quite rapidly.

**The Black Death**
Between 1348 and 1350 the Black Death killed around two-thirds of England's population. It is fourth in terms of numbers who died on Wikipedia's list. The supposed cause of the Black Death was attributed to

astrology and was said to be due to Saturn, Jupiter and Mars being close together; this first occurred in 1345. In astrology a coming together of planets was always a sign of terrible or violent things to come.

The Black Death, also known as bubonic plague, reached England in June 1348 although the term Black Death was not recognised until after the Great Plague preceding the Great Fire of London in the seventeenth century. The first case of the plague was that of a seaman in June 1348; this was centred on Weymouth, Dorset but was thought to have originated in Gascony, France. Medicines at the time were unable to treat the disease.

The Black Death rapidly spread across the south-west of England; Bristol was the first major city to be affected and it then spread to London by late summer of 1348. The full effect of the plague was felt in London in early the following year. Poor ventilation, overcrowded housing and narrow streets flowing with sewage were ideal conditions which allowed the plague to spread rapidly. The environmental conditions were far from ideal and by the spring of 1349 the disease had spread across the whole of southern England. During the first six months of 1349, the whole country was affected, boosted by carriers of the plague arriving on ships docking on Humberside. The Black Death subsided by December 1349 when conditions returned to near normal.

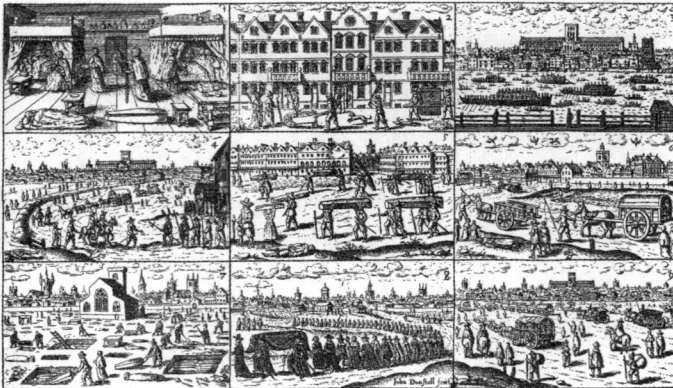

*Scenes typical of life during the Black Death*

A second wave of the plague in 1361–62 caused the death of around twenty per cent of the population. It continued to manifest itself sporadically during the fourteenth and fifteenth centuries but with less severe consequences. The last outbreak of the plague in England to have a significant effect on the population was the Great Plague of London in 1665–1666.

Various methods were used to try and combat the disease including bloodletting, urination and forced vomiting. Sweating was also used as a common treatment; this was achieved using such medicines as *mithridate* and *Venice-treacle* to make the patient sweat violently and purge the blood. If our ancestors suffered from the plague, then the symptoms included the appearance of blotches, glandular hardening and dementia.

In medieval times, lack of medical knowledge forced people to go to extraordinary lengths to try anything to help escape infection – some even whipped themselves hoping that God would forgive their sins and that they would be spared the Black Death. Even poor innocent hapless pigeons were used…

One symptom was the appearance of white and deep swellings; these were anointed with camomile oil which brought them closer to the skin surface and become red in colour in the hope that they were unlikely to come to a head and break. If they did not break, the swellings were broken with a feather from a young pigeon's tail. The tip of the feather was held to the swelling to draw out toxins. If the swelling became black in appearance, the physician would take the young pigeon, cut it open and place the pigeon over the swelling.

## Records and consequences of the Black Death

Although historical records for England were at the time extensive, it was difficult to establish an accurate death toll because of uncertainty about the total population at the time.

The information contained in manorial records provides a good indicator of the geographical spread of the plague and they show that its effect was more or less uniform over all England apart from East Anglia, which was severely affected. Be aware, however, that most manorial records only name the heads of households, normally an adult male. But the manorial records also have Inquisitions Post-Mortem. These documents were sometimes known as *escheats* and were investigations done after the death of a feudal tenant in chief. There are also indications that those most vulnerable to the disease were infants and the elderly. Few fatalities due to the Black Death existed amongst those from higher levels of society.

Many manorial lords suffered labour shortages because of deaths due to the plague so they turned to sheep farming. This compensated for the shortage of manpower because fewer people were needed to work on the land; but as a result of that, arable farming became less popular which added to an insufficiency of basic foods including bread. An inevitable consequence of that was also what we know today as inflation – food generally cost more thus creating even more hardship particularly amongst the poor.

Many settlements declined and some villages were completely abandoned as the population moved to escape the disease and start again. There are few records of those who died as this was before the advent of parish registers; however, the surviving manorial records indicate a loss of between one-third and two-thirds of tenants. Occasionally there are records of specific instances, such as in Canterbury, Kent. Whole villages faced near starvation and towns and cities faced food shortages because the surrounding rural communities could not provide enough food.

Bubonic plagues remained endemic in Britain until the 1660s with the worst epidemics appearing in 1563 and 1603 in London with others elsewhere, particularly in the south-east of England. Occasional references to the effects of the plagues are therefore found in the parish burial registers.

In the immediate aftermath of the Black Death, landowners viewed shortage of labour and the rise in wages as a sign of social upheaval and rebelliousness and they reacted with a degree of oppression. In 1349 the Ordinance of Labourers fixed wages at pre-plague levels and this was reinforced by the Statute of Labourers in 1351. Such laws on labour were ruthlessly enforced in the following decades. Although largely ineffective, the government's measures to enforce the legislation caused huge public resentment and this contributed directly to the Peasants' Revolt in 1381, sometimes referred to as Wat Tyler's Rebellion.

## The Peasants' Revolt 1381

It was the imposition of the unpopular poll tax of 1380 that caused the first popular rebellion in English history – the Peasants' Revolt – although economic discontent had existed for thirty years. The rebellion was supported by well-to-do artisans, manorial villeins, agricultural labourers and the urban working classes.

The revolt was centred in the south-eastern counties and East Anglia, with minor disturbances in other areas of the county beginning in Essex in May 1381. In June rebels from Essex and Kent marched toward London. The Kentish men, led by Wat Tyler, were first to enter London where they massacred some Flemish merchants and razed the Savoy Palace. The government was compelled to negotiate. A day later, the king met the men of Essex at Mile End and promised them cheap land, free trade and the abolition of serfdom and forced labour.

Meanwhile, the Kentish rebels forced the surrender of the Tower of London; what's more, the chancellor and the treasurer who were responsible for the poll tax were beheaded. The king met Wat Tyler and the Kentish men at Smithfield the following day. Tyler was killed by the mayor of London following which the king promised reforms which resulted in the rebels dispersing.

In the provinces the rebellion reached its climax in the following weeks and finally ended when the rebels in East Anglia were defeated by the bishop of Norwich in June. The rebellion lasted less than a month and actually failed completely as a social revolution. The king's promises made at Mile End and Smithfield were forgotten and manorial discontent continued with various local riots taking place from time to time. The rebellion's success, however, did prevent further levying of the poll tax.

## Poll taxes

The poll tax was a lay subsidy, a tax on the movable property of most of the population and it was raised in order to fund wars. It was first levied in 1275 and then continued under various guises until the seventeenth century. The population was taxed on a percentage of the assessed value of their movable goods which varied depending on the year and location. Some were exempt from the tax, including churchmen, the poor, Royal Mint workers, residents of the Cinque Ports, tin workers in Cornwall and those who lived in Cheshire and Durham.

The poll tax of 1379 was graduated according to each taxpayer's rank or social position. The schedule of charges for the tax was divided into four groups based on rank, occupation, civic hierarchy and other men. Two commissions were appointed – one to assess, and the other to collect. This poll tax was expected to bring in over £50,000, but in reality the total was only about £23,000.

The poll taxes of 1377, 1379 and 1381 taxed householders, wives, dependants, and servants individually. The tax records comprise widely varying documents providing information about people who are rarely mentioned in other documents. Large numbers of returns survive; they list the head of the family and their occupations, and some returns provide extremely detailed information about family members as well as servants. Surviving records are held by The National Archives at Kew.

The rebels continued their demands, especially for the abolition of serfdom, and by about 1400, serfdom had become non-existent and was replaced by copyhold tenure. Religious worship was also a victim of the Black Death; many clergymen died so there was a national shortage of priests. Most of the working classes held the parish priest in high regard. The church suggested that the cause of the Black Death was the *impropriety of men* so the people began to lose their faith in the church as so many priests had died … *due to impropriety!* There was also widespread corruption at the time within the Catholic church; this angered many communities so some priests just abandoned their livings. This general dissatisfaction paved the way for the Reformation in England. Deaths due to the Black Death led to a labour shortage and this in turn affected many building projects, especially cathedrals, the construction of which was temporarily halted.

### St Mary's church, Ashwell, Hertfordshire

Although some documentation still exists, it is difficult to envisage what it was like to live through and die as a result of the Black Death. In the nave of Ashwell parish church in Hertfordshire, there is some medieval graffiti on the wall which is thought to have been inscribed by one of the clergymen at the time of the Black Death. It reads as follows:

> there was a plague, 1000, three times 100, five times 10, a pitiable, fierce violent [plague departed]; a wretched populace survives to witness and in the end a mighty wind, Maurus, thunders in this year in the world, 1361.

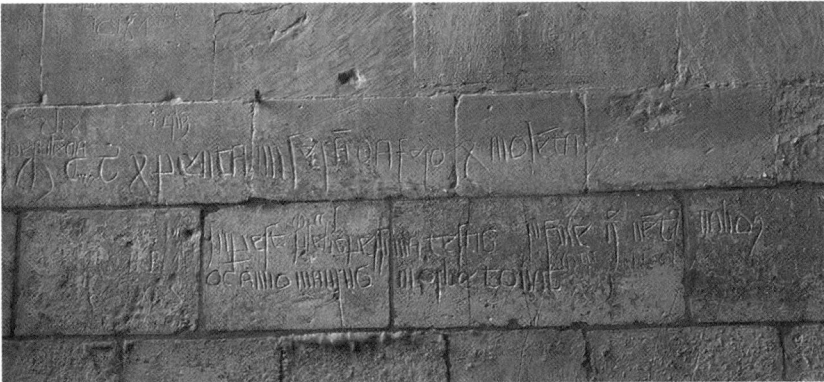

*Medieval graffiti from time of the Black Death in the Church of St Mary the Virgin, Ashwell, Hertfordshire*

The graffiti refers to the *St Maurus Wind*. Records do show that on the 15 January 1362, a terrific storm swept across north-west Europe causing much damage. In England it was known as *The Great Wind* and in Dublin, which was especially badly hit, the *Irish Times* described it as *the Saintly*

*Storm of St Maury's.* Many other medieval buildings including churches were damaged or destroyed throughout the land.

### Charterhouse Square, London

During the Black Death traditional funerals could not be held. In London at the height of the 1348-49 epidemic; hundreds of people were dying from the plague every week forcing parishes to find a practical more cost-effective way of disposing of infected bodies. This invariably meant using plague pits as mass graves. Stretcher-bearers collected the dead bodies during the night and immediately buried them to minimise the risk of further contamination.

One of the largest plague pits was thought to be at Charterhouse Square. In 1371 a Carthusian monastery was founded close to the site, specifically to pray for the souls of the Black Death victims. Although the location of the plague pits cannot be accurately identified, there is a Tudor building standing on the site of the original monastery.

Interestingly, archaeologists working on Crossrail recently discovered a burial site at Farringdon, believed to date around 1349, the height of the Black Death. Records imply there were about 50,000 bodies buried at the pit although only a small number can be identified. The depth of burials and the way the skeletons appear laid out suggests that it was part of a fourteenth-century plague burial ground.

## The medieval leprosy epidemic

Leprosy, known today as Hansen's disease, emerged in England during the fourth century and was endemic by the time of the Norman Conquest. In medieval England leprosy respected no boundaries or class barriers and was seen in both rural and urban communities. Public attitudes towards lepers changed during the fourteenth century when different epidemics including the Black Death led to additional restrictions and isolation. As leprosy began to decrease due to higher levels of immunity within the population, so the established leper houses fell into disuse or were converted into almshouses for the care of the sick and disabled poor.

Most lepers were never cured so they inevitably became permanent inmates; becoming a patient was similar to entering a monastery. New leper patients had to give a substantial amount in "admission money" to help towards hospital costs, so it meant in reality that only a fairly wealthy leper could gain admission. On admission lepers had to take an oath after which they were sprinkled with holy water and then had to kneel at the chapel altar to receive the warden's blessing, thus finalising the admission process.

Many lepers chose to live outside such establishments or were unable to secure accommodation in the units. Informal leper groups often resided in small rural or semi-rural settlements but some remained in their homes and were cared for by their families. Lepers needed to stay involved in society so they could beg for alms, trade and offer other services including praying for the souls of benefactors.

Contracting leprosy meant that victims could suffer loss of fingers and toes, gangrene, blindness, ulcerations, and weakening of bones. In medieval times, religion affected how people felt about the disease; some believed it was a punishment for sin, but others felt that the suffering experienced by lepers was similar to the suffering of Christ. Those who cared for the lepers or made charitable donations believed that their good works would quicken their journey to heaven.

The earliest leper hospital was thought to be St Mary Magdalen in Winchester, Hampshire but at least 300 religious houses and hospitals to care for the lepers were established between the end of the eleventh century and 1350. These were known as *lazar* houses, the name probably deriving from Lazarus who was named in one of Christ's parables. Records of St Mary Magdalen hospital from the thirteenth to seventeenth century are held at the Hampshire archives.

The leper establishments were usually built on the outskirts of towns and cities or in rural areas alongside major travel routes; there was a high demand for places. Most sufferers stayed in touch with their family and social circle and were allowed to make visits home and receive visitors. Most hospitals had a group of cottages surrounding a chapel so that praying and singing could be part of daily life, but changes occurred after the Black Death when fear of infection resulted in additional restrictions and even isolation. These leper houses were often associated with monasteries, but by this time leprosy was beginning to disappear, so gradually the remaining leper houses were used for other purposes such as almshouses which catered for the disabled poor. Indeed, many leper houses were destroyed at the dissolution of the monasteries.

The topic of almshouses is covered at length in volume one of this series, so what follows is just a brief resume of almshouses. The inmates or residents of almshouses were called bedesmen or bedeswomen; *bede* means prayer and *bedehouses* were distinguished from hospitals and almshouses by the fact that they were founded specifically so that the poor might spend the rest of their lives in grateful prayer for the souls of their benefactors. Admittedly this was something which was often required in medieval almshouses and hospitals but that wasn't the sole reason for their foundation whereas with *bedehouses*, the resident priest was assured of a captive audience!

The bedehouse was a dwelling place for twelve men over fifty years of age to live in 'close company' with one woman to look after them. Each man had a little cubicle with a locker, divided off by a screen from his fellows, and the rest of the hall formed a common room with an open fireplace.

By the early fifteenth century, many hospitals were deteriorating rapidly, corruption was rife and absentee masters lived at the expense of the hospital funds for long periods of time. This then resulted in the foundation of some exceptionally well-endowed hospitals and bedehouses plus an increase in almshouses of secular origin because men had begun to look to their own needs with little dependence on the Church. The dissolution of the monasteries and the Reformation had a profound effect on many of the charitable foundations. There were no new hospitals or almshouses built in England for more than thirty years. Many of the poor who were already living in such foundations were evicted and found themselves on the streets.

## Smallpox epidemics

Prior to the sixteenth century smallpox was a minor disease in Britain but a century later it was quite common. The disease was first known as the *pox* or the *red plague*. At the time smallpox was one of our ancestors' greatest fears. Within one or two weeks of being exposed to smallpox, sufferers experienced fever, chills, headache, nausea, vomiting and severe muscle aches; the fever decreased after which a rash appeared. People were infectious once the rash appeared and until the scab of the pox fell off. The rash began as flat or slightly raised spots which enlarged and were filled initially with fluid then pus.

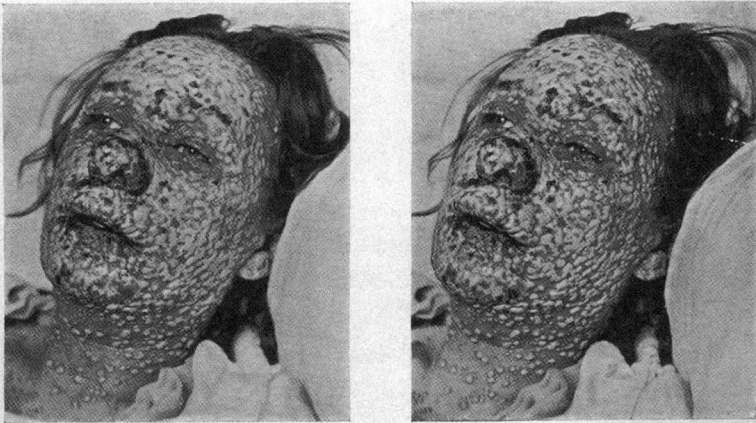

PLATE LIII.

An example of unmodified confluent smallpox. The eruption was beyond the height of its maturity and the swelling of the features was subsiding.

*Woman suffering smallpox. Pustular eruption of smallpox on face*

Smallpox was a major killer during the late seventeenth and eighteenth centuries; it was especially virulent in overcrowded cities and amongst the infant generation. But the disease also reached into rural areas affecting

21

young adults. A fifth of all deaths in the eighteenth century were in some way or other attributable to smallpox. Those who survived smallpox were scarred and pockmarked; this was something which troubled ladies more as it might reduce their marriage potential, so they began to wear patches known as beauty spots to hide their facial scars. Society began to accept vaccination following Jenner's discovery and the procedure gained immense popularity. During the nineteenth century, one-third of all the cases of blindness were caused by smallpox. Up to sixty per cent of those infected died; the death rate amongst children was about eighty per cent.

In Britain widespread epidemics of smallpox have occurred over time.

- 1751–1753 – the first epidemic and smallpox became more common
- 1796 – this epidemic resulted in over 38,500 deaths
- 1816–1819 – epidemic began in central England and spread rapidly to London, Canterbury, Nottinghamshire, Staffordshire and throughout East Anglia
- 1825–1826 – the first national epidemic with the poorer population suffering most, yet the most likely group to avoid vaccination
- 1837–1840 – the epidemic killed around 42,000. It started in south-west and spread throughout Wales and then to the industrial north-west
- 1871–1872 – this outbreak resulted in around 42,000 deaths mainly amongst adults. It is believed to have been spread by refugees entering England to escape the French-Prussian conflicts
- 1901–1902 – this was the last epidemic to affect the British Isles.

Death from smallpox was often recorded as such in parish registers. Burials for those who died of smallpox were exempt from duties imposed under the various Burial in Woollen Acts which existed until 1814, although generally ignored after 1770. Under normal conditions an affidavit had to be sworn in front of a Justice of the Peace by a relative of the deceased confirming burial in wool. A £5 fine could be imposed for noncompliance. Burial entries in parish registers were usually marked with the word *affidavit* or similar as official confirmation that an affidavit had been sworn.

Alternatively, the burial entry would be marked *naked* for those too poor to afford the woollen shroud. That terminology was sometimes used to denote a smallpox death as well.

## Cholera epidemics

Prior to 1830, cholera was known as *English cholera* or *summer diarrhoea* and the diagnosis could include any acute intestinal disorder. After 1830 the virulent *Asiatic cholera* reached England resulting in the first pandemic in 1832 when 52,000 died; the first case was in Sunderland. A second outbreak in 1848-9 resulted in the deaths of 53,293 people, and there was another epidemic between 1852 and 1853.

Cholera is a waterborne disease caused by contaminated drinking water and the most common symptoms included nausea, dizziness, diarrhoea, insatiable thirst and cramps. It spread rapidly amongst the poor communities and the regular advice given to them was to avoid alcohol, eat moderately and empty their bowels to stop any vomiting and diarrhoea. These so-called treatments further weakened those suffering from cholera and made them even more dehydrated, thus accelerating fatal consequences. Sometimes patients were treated with camphor and mercury or bled with leeches. Death due to dehydration, lethargy, erratic heartbeat, sunken eyes and dry and shrivelled skin usually followed within a day or two after the first symptoms appeared. It was estimated that 2,000 people a week were dying in England in the late 1840s due to cholera. Doctors had no idea how the disease spread and there was no known cure.

The first cholera outbreak in 1831 was followed by epidemics of influenza and typhoid in the 1830s prompting the government to commission public health reformer, Edwin Chadwick, to carry out an enquiry into standards of sanitation. In his 1842 report – *The Sanitary Conditions of the Labouring Population* – Edwin Chadwick showed that there was an undisputed connection between poor living conditions, diseases and general life expectancy. His investigation culminated with the 1848 Public Health Act which established the Board of Health to provide advice on disease prevention and

*Cholera treatment equipment: portable apparatus for injecting saline solution*

made arrangements for local health boards across the country, each with a medical officer to investigate sanitary conditions locally. However, the compulsory appointment of a Medical Officer of Health in each locality only occurred after 1872 although many areas had appointed a person soon after the local board of health was established.

The medical officers for each local board were required to send reports with full details of each person contracting the disease and other matters relevant to general public health to the Board of Health. Records can be researched at The National Archives in series MH13. Besides the Board of Health, the Metropolitan Sewers Commission was created in 1848 to oversee the connection of houses to the main sewerage system within the London area.

# CHAPTER 3

# OCCUPATIONAL DISEASES

The occupations followed by many of our ancestors were more varied in nature than those of today. There were more manual labouring jobs until mechanisation took over and this is especially true in rural and agricultural areas. In larger urban areas, industrialisation happened more quickly but also gave rise to more jobs. No matter what occupation our ancestors followed, there is no doubt that their actual jobs could have contributed in the longer term to their deaths.

Poor nutrition and living conditions, dirty and difficult working situations all added to a shorter lifespan in those days. Causes of disease were medically unknown and some occupational diseases did not result in death but had a long-term effect on general health.

## Anthrax

Anthrax is also known as *wool-sorter's disease*; it was first encountered in England in 1847 amongst sheep, but the people employed in various trades associated with animals such as slaughtering, working with the hair or wool of infected animals and curriers of the skins also became infected. Person-to-person transmission was rare. Treatments for anthrax were introduced in the early twentieth century, but before that, anthrax usually led to septicaemia which resulted ultimately in death. Anthrax has now been virtually eliminated using vaccines and antibiotic treatment.

## Mad hatter's disease

The medical term for mad hatter's disease is erethism (*erethismus mercurialis*); it is a **neurological disease** caused by mercury poisoning. Hatters were particularly affected because they worked with mercury in the hat-making process – a chemical called mercuric nitrate was used to stiffen felt for hats and, because most of their workshops were poorly ventilated, the hatters couldn't help but inhale mercury vapours on a daily basis. Many developed chronic mercury poisoning which manifested itself as psychosis, with loss of weight, impaired speech and tremors. These symptoms gave rise to the phrase *mad as a hatter*. Mercury poisoning also took its toll of other workers such as those who silvered mirrors and the gilders who applied gold and mercury to metal.

## Silicosis – stonecutters' phthisis

Silicosis is a disease caused by inhaling dust from silica; it is also known as stonecutters' phthisis and pulmonic disease. This affliction was very common amongst potters, miners, sand-blasters and stonemasons. A similar condition known as siderosis or *grinders' rot* was caused by the inhalation of metallic particles; siderosis also affected cutlers, surgical instrument-makers and saw-makers, all of whom worked with silica.

The bronchial symptoms of silicosis and siderosis were similar to tuberculosis and so the disease was often incorrectly diagnosed. If a workshop was part of a home environment, then it was possible that other members of a worker's family, particularly young children, could suffer from the disease too as the particles were airborne. Anyone following an occupation where they were continually exposed to fine dust particles could contract similar diseases with the same consequences.

## Phthisis, consumption and tuberculosis

A common cause of death seen on death certificates was phthisis. It was the term used by most Victorian medical practitioners to describe pulmonary tuberculosis. Using the word *phthisis* allowed a degree of consistency and it eventually became standard terminology as directed by the registrar general when someone died of pulmonary tuberculosis.

Phthisis or consumption was a widespread killer throughout history; there are even references to it as a fatal disease amongst the ancient Greeks. They named the disease of the lungs phthisis or consumption owing to the rapid loss of weight that consumed the individual as the disease progressed. It has been a major killer over the past two or three centuries.

At the beginning of the nineteenth century, doctors were unsure whether tuberculosis was an infectious or a hereditary disease or even a cancer. In the nineteenth and early twentieth century, consumption was a major fear and caused great concern amongst the population. It was seen as an endemic disease particularly among the urban poor. Four million people died from tuberculosis in England and Wales between 1851 and the start of the First World War with more than one third of them aged between fifteen and thirty-five years of age.

A person infected with tuberculosis was unlikely to show any immediate symptoms; those with a healthy immune system, good nutrition and a clean air environment usually only slightly suffered and eventually overcame the disease. But people in the lower classes were more likely to have weakened immune systems due to poor nutrition and ill health. During the first few years of civil registration between 1837 and 1841, statistics show that between a quarter and a third of tradesmen and manual labourers died from tuberculosis. In the upper classes, the number dying from tuberculosis was significantly less because affected wealthy people often travelled to areas with mild climates in an attempt to overcome the disease.

In the early stages when people showed no signs or symptoms, the disease was almost dormant and individuals were not contagious. But over time as the disease became active, people developed the symptoms and ultimately became contagious. The transition from latent to active usually took only a few weeks, but it could also occur years later. About half the people who developed the disease did so within the first two years of infection and those affected died about three years later.

Symptoms included chest pain, fever, severe weight loss and a cough producing sputum or blood. During the nineteenth century, there were no reliable treatments; some physicians prescribed bleeding and purging though most could only advise sufferers to rest, eat well, and exercise outdoors. Very few people fully recovered but if any survived the first round of the disease, they invariably suffered from recurrences which affected their future lifestyle often resulting in death.

The first recorded treatment for consumption was in the early nineteenth century. James Carson, an English doctor, demonstrated that injecting air into the pleural cavity could cause a lung to collapse which allowed it to heal. In 1882 the bacillus causing tuberculosis was finally identified. The practice of collapsing a lung became the initial treatment although it did not work for those who were suffering advanced stages of the disease. It wasn't until the mid-1940s that antibiotics became the effective treatment and cure.

## Sanatorium care

The first sanatorium for the treatment of tuberculosis was at Brompton Hospital which opened in 1854. Tuberculosis was fatal in the early days; it was not identified as an infectious disease until the mid-1860s. By the end of the nineteenth century many private sanatoriums existed but after the 1921 Public Health Act, local authorities began to build sanatoriums.

Until the early 1950s treatment for tuberculosis was generally undertaken in a sanatorium, a facility for long-term illness, and this was usually the only option available for poorer patients although the wealthier often went to other institutions for treatment. Patients in the sanatorium were required to work and be responsible for their own housekeeping. Those infected with the disease who did not go to a sanatorium coped at home, often sleeping outside. The use of sanatoriums led to improved outcomes for patients; in the thirty years after their establishment, deaths from tuberculosis were almost halved in England and Wales.

Immediately after admission to a sanatorium, patients spent the first few days in bed under close medical observation. A typical day started at 7.30 am with breakfast at 8.30 am followed by work. There would be a short break for rest and lunch and during the afternoon patients were encouraged to go for walks. Afternoon tea was taken around 4.30pm followed immediately by board games or other pastimes until the evening meal. Afterwards entertainment including concerts or talks may have been arranged. The spiritual needs of patients were taken care of by local clerics of various denominations. Many sanatoriums had their own library and patients were encouraged to read. Bedtime was usually around 9 pm preceded by a milky bedtime drink which was considered essential to healing.

The food in sanatoriums was generous and in accordance with medical opinion on the treatment of tuberculosis. The importance of fresh air was also emphasized. Patients were accommodated in pavilions or chalet-style wards exposed to fresh air twenty-four hours a day – unless they were situated in exposed areas where snow or rain could blow in; even in such instances there was still fresh air circulation from open windows. Some sanatoriums also had solariums, known as sun balconies. Some sanatoriums also had solariums so the patients were able to have a daily swim. Smoking was discouraged in most sanatoriums but it was never totally banned. The medical philosophy at the time was that smoking in the fresh air was not detrimental to a patient's health. Alcohol, however, was not allowed.

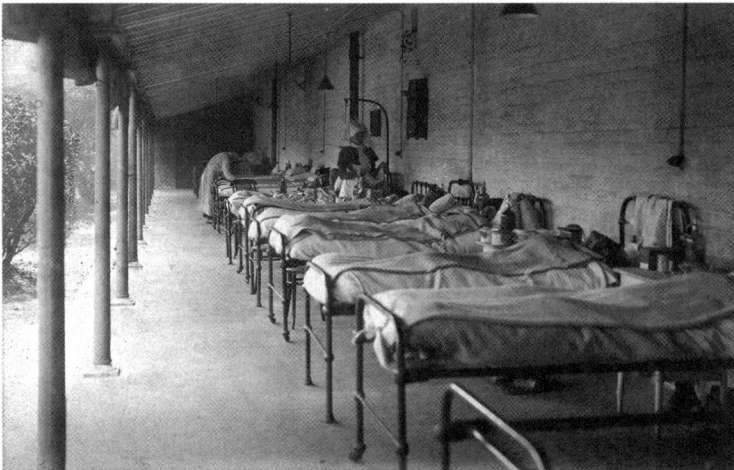

*Open air tuberculosis ward at the Royal Hospital Haslar*

Most sanatoriums had a work programme for their patients, with jobs undertaken being dependent upon their fitness levels. The fittest patients carried out heavy work. Work was not compulsory but patients were encouraged to take part and their progress was monitored as they transferred from one grade of work to another. Patients normally stayed in sanatoriums for between four and six months and most of those discharged in a satisfactory condition would remain so and be permanently cured, provided they continued the regime of plenty of fresh air, good food and a suitable occupation.

During WWII miniature radiography, a form of diagnostic imaging, helped enormously in the examination of large groups of service personnel and war workers. In Britain, the Royal Navy and Royal Air Force led the way but it was not until 1943 that routine screening of civilians began and it was the late 1950s when mass radiography proved to be invaluable.

# CHAPTER 4

# COMMON VICTORIAN DISEASES 1837–1900

In 1837 at the beginning of Queen Victoria's reign, birth and death registration became compulsory. In addition, it was also the period when the censuses between 1841 and 1901 required more information from householders and this in turn made them quite significant research documents for family historians. From a medical point of view, the best and most useful document is the death certificate.

## Death certificates

Analysing an ancestor's death certificate does not always provide a true picture of the actual cause of death. This was particularly true for deaths registered before medical certification became a requirement. It is often easy to determine the cause by investigating what was happening in the locality and whether there were any apparent epidemics, contagious diseases rampant at the time, natural disasters or mine and industrial accidents. Besides death certificates, there were often notes made in parish burial registers or local newspapers about the circumstances surrounding death.

Although the causes of death were not always clearly defined, a significant number of causes were also recorded as "unknown". Many deaths occurred because of infectious disease. Infant and childhood mortality was high because of the common childhood infections. Some deaths of children under five years old resulted from diarrhoea which, along with dysentery and typhoid, also contributed to deaths among adults. Tuberculosis or consumption was responsible for the high death rate particularly among young adults. Most cardiac problems were as a consequence of infectious diseases although heart disease was well-recognised and was generally associated with wealthier overweight men who were basically idle.

The causes of death can provide the researcher with a fascinating insight into which diseases were prevalent within a community and how the causes were described over time. You will probably come across many unfamiliar words because of the archaic medical terminology used at the time; nevertheless, knowing these words and terms will still help you to understand the advances made in medical knowledge during the Victorian era and beyond. (See glossary.)

Obviously, sparsely populated areas generally showed fewer deaths from food and waterborne gastro-intestinal infections than large urban centres of people. Waterborne diseases and those caused by bad or rotting food were widespread in many communities because sanitary conditions were far from ideal. This factor also contributed to high infant and childhood mortality. In Victorian Britain, the accuracy of death certification was not perfect but it improved when the Births and Deaths Registration Act of 1874 tightened the loopholes. The doctor looking after someone during their last illness was required to certify the cause of death. All doubtful cases had to be referred to the coroner. This meant that both prime and contributory conditions were recorded as the cause of death.

Poor rural communities actually enjoyed the best diet and health in Victorian times because their food was obtained locally and they lived a more traditional lifestyle. Unfortunately, these rural communities gradu-ally began to disappear because of urbanisation, more modern farming methods being introduced and population migration. In the aftermath of the Industrial Revolution, such changes were inevitable. However, in many of Britain's urban areas, improvements in living conditions, better transport links and easier access to imported foods led to a longer life expectancy.

Arrangements for sewage disposal were at best rudimentary; in some towns the streets contained open sewers which caused a huge risk to people's health. The Victorian census returns give researchers a clear snapshot so we can understand the overcrowded conditions encountered daily by our ancestors. Censuses frequently show large families living in a couple of rooms or several families residing in the same house. These urban areas were dreadfully overcrowded; very basic cramped washing facilities would be shared by many households, as was the single toilet – and it was not a flushing one! Such conditions did nothing to curtail the spread of infection or disease.

The urban development resulting from industrialisation meant that nineteenth-century towns and cities were prone to all types of disease. Due to high death rates, urban burial grounds became overcrowded. Many churchyards had existed for centuries and many of the graves were re-used by burying one body on top of another. It was quite common for bones to be visible at or around ground level and this created both an unwholesome atmosphere and a real health risk, so much so that many churchyards were closed to new burials from the mid-1850s – many by the new sanitary inspectors appointed after 1866.

There were several Burial Acts between 1852 and 1885 because burial grounds were just running out of space so some regulation was necessary. The Burial Acts of 1852 for London and 1853 for the rest of the country paved the way to help overcome the problem of overcrowded burial grounds – in mainly urban areas. Most overcrowded churchyards were closed to further burials. Private enterprise and local authorities set up and ran public cemeteries. Local authority cemeteries were managed by burial boards. The governing legislation was consolidated in 1857. Some private cemeteries existed prior to the Burial Acts so many people already accepted the concept of burial in a cemetery rather than a churchyard. Further provision was made for the disposal of the dead and in March 1885, the first cremation was carried out at Woking, Surrey at the crematorium adjacent to Brookwood cemetery.

*Bunhill Fields London – typical overcrowded burial ground.*

So what exactly were the causes of our ancestors' deaths? Was death because of an epidemic, an accident or something more sinister or unusual? Was the cause recorded as a result of a proper clinical diagnosis? Let us examine some of the more common, and not so common, causes and their circumstances.

Many common diseases and ailments, if left untreated or treated incorrectly, had fatal consequences. Some of these diseases by their very nature, developed into uncontrollable epidemics which left the medical profession unable to cope because they did not fully understand the diagnosis or have access to suitable treatments. It was regrettable that no action had been taken to improve sanitation and waste problems.

## Diarrhoea

Diarrhoea was a symptom of other diseases but was accepted as a principal cause of infant deaths in the Victorian period; death due to diarrhoea was widespread in poorer homes where there was little attention paid to hygiene. Poor food and an unhealthy diet didn't help either. *Calomel* was commonly used to eradicate diarrhoea but because it was a purgative, it was the wrong treatment. It is thought that up to fifty per cent of illegitimate children died from the disease within their first year because they were weaned too early – the single mother needed to return to work. Some infants were also given drugs such as opium or laudanum to enable their mothers to sleep which only added to the complications. On death certificates many deaths from cholera were incorrectly recorded as being from diarrhoea.

## Cancer

In the eighteenth century cancer was regarded as a female disorder because the common cancers affecting the breasts and cervix were obvious to the medical profession. However, most cancers throughout the Victorian era were misdiagnosed as consumption (TB) or old age; as late as 1883, fatal blood loss due to cervical cancer in post-menopausal women was diagnosed as *menstruation of old age* – a recorded cause of death which was common.

British surgeon Percival Pott first identified cancer as early as 1775. It was cancer of the scrotum which was found to be a common disease among chimney sweeps and more specifically their climbing boys. Scientists discovered that cancer spread from the prime tumour to other areas of the body through the lymph nodes. This discovery was formulated by English surgeon, Campbell de Morgan, in the early 1870s. Surgery like other procedures was initially not that effective but as medical science developed, surgery became the primary treatment for cancer; success was dependent on the skill of the individual surgeon at removing a tumour and equally important, removing sufficient tissue surrounding the tumour to prevent the spread. When Marie Curie discovered radiation towards the end of the nineteenth century, she had found the first effective non-surgical cancer treatment. Hospital radiologists began to work with patients to shrink tumours and reduce the risk of the cancer spreading.

During the nineteenth century, the only treatment was to surgically remove the tumour, but invasive surgery was not always successful. In fact this type of surgery almost guaranteed death; if a patient survived, it took years for them to recover or left them with debilitating ailments.

Many people resorted to quack remedies which were even less effective but they were widely used. Doctors thought that purging and bloodletting were essential in the treatment of cancer. Even more bizarre was the use of substances such as caustic soda or hydrochloric acid which would have been very painful and had little or no effect. Many other treatments were applied to the skin around the site of the tumour or were taken by mouth including arsenic, cyanide and poisonous plant extracts. New treatments began to emerge in the late nineteenth century including the use of X-ray technology and radiotherapy.

We are all familiar with the term chemotherapy these days. Chemotherapy uses medicine to kill the cancer cells and had its origins in the chemical warfare sector during the Second World War. Mustard gas as used during WWI had existed for years but to some extent it was a medical mystery. Scientists knew that cancer cells multiplied much faster than normal cells so they wondered if a low dose of nitrogen mustard could be used to treat cancer. Cyclophosphamide was the active element in nitrogen mustard and the first time a cancer patient was treated with it, the tumour shrank which was not thought possible at the time. Thus chemotherapy was born. However, this all proved to be a temporary marvel because the treatment had to be stopped as the side effects were regarded as life-threatening.

## Effects of alcohol

Beer was often safer to drink than water so it is not surprising that the poorer classes sometimes drank to excess. Many manual workers drank beer for refreshment during their working day as a matter of course – indeed some employers provided a beer allowance as part of their workers' wages. Some workers brewed their own beer or could obtain jugs of ale cheaply from the local outdoor beerhouses. Many workplace accidents happened because excess alcohol impaired a worker's ability to operate machinery, but although not directly noted as the cause of death, consumption of

alcohol led to untimely deaths. In those days, employers were not interested in the remedies and often sacked workers for drunkenness.

The wealthier classes also drank but their choice was wine or spirits; but
these could lead to sclerosis and other alcohol-related problems, some of
which resulted in organ failure and premature death if not detected and
treated.

In the 1880s cocaine was regularly used to treat alcoholism as it was
thought it dulled the craving. Cocaine was also used as a cure for morphine
addiction, depression, anxiety, fatigue, and migraines. It was available as
powders, in wines and as a soft drink. The alternatives were widely publi-
cised by the end of the century and included slowly sucking an orange or
drinking hot water.

## Lead poisoning

With the Industrial Revolution and the expansion of towns and cities, the
domestic water supply was provided through lead piping; as the water
flowed through the pipes, it picked up deadly toxins on its journey between
reservoir and dwellings. In 1847 and 1848, the government imposed laws
against the pollution of drinking water but the effects of water passing
through lead were unknown at the time. Lead was also added to paint to
make the colours more vivid and to prevent early deterioration.

The Victorians used lead paint on their furniture, cots, and children's toys.
Some toys like toy soldiers were actually moulded from lead because it was
malleable but when children chewed on toys, they were in fact sadly slowly
poisoning themselves.

Long-term exposure to lead resulted in serious medical conditions which
could cause ultimate death. People who were smelters, plumbers, painters,
stained-glass window glaziers, paper-stainers and potters were all susceptible to an early death caused by lead poisoning due to their occupation.
The effects of lead poisoning were often slow to materialise and sufferers
encountered ailments such as colic, anaemia, blindness and forms of
paralysis.

# Diphtheria

At the beginning of the 1800s diphtheria was a rare disease and was not easily differentiated from other ulcer-based throat diseases until the early 1820s. It was a common childhood infectious disease and became a major cause of death in children even into the early twentieth century. It was also known as the *kiss disease*. Diphtheria symptoms became apparent between two to seven days after initial infection and they included fever, chills, fatigue, a sore throat, hoarseness, cough, headache, difficult or painful swallowing, rapid breathing and blood-stained nasal discharge. It consequently destroyed healthy tissue within the respiratory system.

On death certificates prior to 1874, diphtheria was often shown as *strangling angel*, *Egyptian ulcer* and *plague of the throat*. Before 1858 outbreaks of the disease were not common but were most prevalent in the east of England. In some cases death from diphtheria was wrongly diagnosed and recorded as croup; some doctors also confused it with tonsillitis or scarlet fever. Human-to-human airborne transmission and infection occurred when an infected individual coughed, sneezed or kissed someone. Indirect infections were also known to occur. Even when an infected individual touched a surface or object, the bacteria was often left behind and remained active.

If any of your ancestors died as a result of diphtheria, they may have endured an uncomfortable, possibly even a slow death because of the gradual progression of the disease. In severe cases patients also developed pneumonia or respiratory failure which would have led to suffocation which would have been recorded as the true cause of death with diphtheria appearing as a secondary or contributing cause.

Many Victorian families resorted to more old-fashioned natural remedies such as using syrup made from hyacinth flowers, and some nurses recommended gargling with potassium chlorate and water. One of the biggest fears was that the disease would progress beyond a throat infection to the blood which could lead to possible organ failure which would be fatal.

Towards the end of the nineteenth century, patients were usually transferred to isolation hospitals to keep them away from others and reduce the possibility of further infections. Later in the twentieth century, vaccinations became available which considerably reduced the instances of diphtheria in the population.

## Influenza

Influenza in its various forms has killed thousands in the past. The worst outbreak was just after First World War when half the world's population was infected and it caused around thirty million deaths which was more than the total number killed during the First World War battles and conflicts. Known as the *Spanish Flu of 1918* it was considered to be one of the greatest disasters since the plagues of the 1300s.

The virus was spread by soldiers returning home from the trenches of northern France. The troops travelled home by train and as they arrived at the railway stations, the infection spread from the stations throughout the cities, their suburbs and even to the countryside. People became ill with symptoms including sore throats, headaches and a loss of appetite. Although flu was highly infectious within the wartime trenches, recovery was fairly quick and it became known amongst soldiers as the *three-day fever.*

The first recorded outbreak of flu was in Glasgow in May 1918 when many young women, especially those working in factories, were worst affected. The flu reached London in June and infected the whole country by October. Young adults between twenty and thirty years of age were particularly affected and the disease struck and progressed quickly in these cases, sometimes within twenty-four hours.

The onset of flu was very quick and within hours of feeling the first symptoms, many people developed pneumonia and suffocated to death. Around a quarter of the British population were affected and the death toll in Britain reached 228,000. During the last summer of the First World War, government efforts were focused on ending the conflict rather than dealing with or controlling the pandemic. The records of the registrar general showed that the towns of Hebburn, Jarrow, Barnsley and Wallsend suffered the worst rates of deaths.

A shortage of undertakers and gravediggers led to infected bodies remaining unburied for longer than normal with many funerals taking place at night. Local authorities and newspapers published advice recommending people to stop shaking hands and to give up kissing. These and many other measures were implemented using information posters. Health visitors and school nurses undertook door-to-door leaflet drops and recommended that infected people remained isolated and go to bed as soon as symptoms became apparent. They were also advised to gargle with potash and salt.

Eventually, schools closed and cinemas and theatres were required to ventilate the buildings for thirty minutes every three hours and all shows began with public information films. Churches remained open because people were encouraged to turn to religion and not be prevented from worshipping. It was also business as usual in most industries. Public parades were also allowed to happen.

Huge numbers of medical professionals and volunteers treated the wounded and injured on the battlefields in WWI and many remained on the front lines during the epidemic. Back in England the remaining medics had to deal with treating the flu but many did not appreciate the severity of the disease. The *British Medical Journal* suggested that the *inconvenience of flu should be quietly borne*. It was not until the summer of 1919 that the flu pandemic subsided.

## Measles

Measles was a highly contagious infection which led to many deaths resulting from its complications. It could lay dormant between major outbreaks, meaning that little if any immunity was built up by infants born since the previous outbreak. Cramped and overcrowded living conditions typical of the Victorian urban environment allowed the virus to spread quickly; many victims died of complications including meningitis and pneumonia. It was not until the introduction of a vaccine in the early twentieth century that measles began to be controlled.

## Scarlet fever

Scarlet fever caused many deaths among young children, regardless of social class; it was frequently attributed to drinking milk that was processed at infected dairies. The disease was spread through respiratory droplets from children rather than infants. There were several epidemics in the Victorian period and between 1825 and 1885, outbreaks regularly occurred usually with fatal consequences. Throughout the mid-nineteenth century, mortality rates as a result of scarlet fever hit a peak in England and Wales.

In north-west England, there was a high mortality rate in many major cities where babies were not expected to live beyond young adulthood. During the 1860s in many northern industrial towns, life expectancy was less than thirty-five years. The reduction in deaths from scarlet fever occurred after the identification of streptococcus in the 1880s although effective treatments were not widely available until the interwar years of the twentieth century.

Scarlet fever was also referred to as *scarlatina*. Although it was mainly a childhood ailment, it affected people of all ages. Its name was derived from the telltale red skin rash. Before antibiotics, the disease caused lengthy periods of illness, other complications, and death. Children with scarlet fever were immediately isolated or quarantined.

## Sexually-transmitted diseases

Syphilis, also referred to as the French pox, was widespread throughout the nineteenth and early twentieth century. Many patients were infected and became deaf, blind, disorientated or suffered from jaundice. General paralysis often occurred during the late stages of the illness which often resulted in a term in an asylum.

Obviously the disease was closely associated with the sex trade and prostitutes who caught syphilis spread it via their clients to their wives, other mistresses and even to children. Those who had syphilis or any other sexually-transmitted disease could be forcibly detained for treatment. In the late 1860s the Contagious Diseases Acts attempted to control sexually-transmitted diseases in the military and naval communities by prohibiting prostitution in garrison towns and ports. The Ladies' National Association, a protest movement, campaigned on the basis that the problem was that it was the men who frequented prostitutes that should be punished – not the prostitutes. Their campaign resulted in the original Acts being suspended in 1883 and finally repealed by 1886.

Syphilis was difficult to cure because those infected thought the disease had disappeared or they had been cured, only to be affected by a later recurrence of the symptoms. However, patients who responded to treatment were normally given a clean bill of health by their doctors.

During the nineteenth century when a patient was diagnosed with syphilis, doctors believed that this caused despair and gloominess in the patient which then caused infertility, miscarriages and stillbirths. Children born to infected mothers sometimes never showed any signs of infection, whereas others may have died in infancy or developed serious health complications. Unfortunately, during the nineteenth century, infection among wives and children was very common irrespective of social class.

Many infected wives struggled whereas their husbands were effectively protected by the medical and legal establishment. If a husband infected his wife with a sexually-transmitted disease, the doctors were required to conceal the cause of her illness; doctors used the excuse of patient confidentiality and if they disclosed the fact to a wife, she would immediately know that her husband had been unfaithful and contracted syphilis.

In the mid-nineteenth century, the medical authorities were convinced that prostitutes were the main cause of the infection; however, by the 1890s public criticism shifted to the idea that upper-class men were exploiting working-class women and by doing so infected their own families.

Mercury was used in the treatment of syphilis, usually administered in heavy doses resulting in severe mercury poisoning. Mercury poisoning caused the same symptoms as seen in the late stage of syphilis, so many doctors continued to administer mercury injections until penicillin replaced mercury in the late 1920s. Mercury was not the only treatment used; iodide treatments were also available but they were not as popular. Lotions were often applied to decrease inflammations and normal hygiene rituals such as shaving and bathing were also necessary.

While syphilis could be fatal, other sexually-transmitted diseases also required intensive medical treatment often involving a stay in hospital and could be cured or at least their progression was halted. There was also a common myth in the late 1800s that men suffering from syphilis were cured by having sex with a young virgin girl, who when indulging in the sex act, would effectively take the disease from them. Despite the supposed Victorian high moral code, it was known that there were more brothels operating than schools! Around 80,000 women of all ages were engaged in prostitution in the late 1800s, many recording their occupation as "actress"!

### Single woman's churchyard – "Bishop of Winchester's geese"
The Cross Bones Graveyard in Southwark was a post-medieval cemetery which was the final resting place for more than 15,000 poor and destitute Londoners including a large number of prostitutes who had been licensed by the Bishop of Winchester. The first reference to the graveyard was in 1598 when the *Survey of London* referred to it as a *Single Woman's Churchyard* which at the time became a euphemism for a prostitute.

Southwark, part of the Bishop of Winchester's London estates, had been known over the centuries as an area where most of the residents were poor. It had the reputation as London's pleasure garden where popular pastimes such as bearbaiting took place as did otherwise banned theatrical performances. The *Bishop of Winchester's Geese*, the name by which local prostitutes were known, plied their trade in brothels scattered throughout the area.

Although the prostitutes were licensed by the bishop, they were not allowed to be buried in consecrated ground so non-consecrated land was

*Cross Bones burial ground, Southwark*

made available at the burial ground, located south of Southwark Cathedral. By 1769 the graveyard was being used to bury the poor of St Saviour's parish as well the prostitutes and a number of criminals. The burial ground became very overcrowded, resulting in the parish authorities complaining that the graveyard was so full that new bodies had to be buried within two feet of the surface. The air pollution from rotting corpses was blamed for a cholera outbreak in the 1830s although in reality the cause related to the impure water supply. Like other churchyards in London, Cross Bones became so overcrowded that it constituted a public health concern and burials were stopped in 1853.

## Typhoid

Typhoid, also known as enteric fever, was contracted through drinking or washing in contaminated water. Because of poor or non-existent sewage treatment, people were regularly drinking and using infected water. Typhoid was then spread by asymptomatic carriers. Although it developed more slowly than cholera, it was inevitably fatal.

It was often inappropriately treated with purgatives resulting in death for most sufferers. The medical professions often confused typhoid with typhus; this was due to just plain lack of knowledge. Between 1830 and the 1860s, typhoid claimed many lives particularly among the poor. The most tragic death in Victorian times due to typhoid was that of Prince Albert who died in 1861.

There was no effective medication or treatment until 1897 when Almroth Edward Wright developed an effective vaccination regime for treating typhoid. In 1892 he was appointed professor of pathology at the Royal Army Medical College, Netley where he worked on a method of immuni- sation against typhoid fever. In 1898 he was in India as a member of the Plague Commission and in 1902 he was a pathologist at St. Mary's Hospital, London where he used vaccines extensively for the treatment of typhoid and other bacterial infections.

By the end of the nineteenth century, knowledge of how the disease was caused and why it spread had improved considerably; the government had passed various Public Health Acts, vaccinations were becoming available and people practised better personal hygiene.

## Typhus fever

Typhus was an endemic disease spread by body lice and rat fleas. Fleas, mites, lice, and ticks all carried the disease. When any of these insects bit someone, they easily transmitted the bacteria that caused typhus. The bites itched intensively and people instinctively scratched them; this in turn opened the skin and allowed the bacteria access to the bloodstream. Once in the bloodstream, the bacteria reproduced and grew.

Typhus symptoms included rose-coloured spots, exhaustion, weakness and sometimes delirium. There were regular outbreaks amongst military personnel involved in war. It was also prevalent amongst the poor who lived in overcrowded and unsanitary conditions in urban areas.

Typhus was endemic in London and epidemics also occurred in many other towns; the epidemic in 1865 killed over 10,000 people in London alone. Ireland was also affected with a major epidemic during the Irish Famine between 1846 and 1849. The Irish strain of typhus was brought into to England where it became known as *Irish fever* and killed many people of all social classes.

## Whooping cough

Whooping cough had existed since the Middle Ages although evidence suggests it could possibly have occurred earlier. In the mid-1600s it was known by its medical name *pertussis* which means intensive cough. This disease was often referred to as *chin cough,* associated with the strange sounding whoop of a cough which often induced vomiting. It was highly contagious in younger children and often resulted in pneumonia and bronchitis. On average, whooping cough killed around 1,000 young children each year.

In the eighteenth and nineteenth centuries, doctors disagreed over the treatment of whooping cough, but it was distinguishable enough to be recorded in the London Bills of Mortality. Outbreaks of whooping cough became a regular occurrence throughout the country. Between 1844 and 1853 it was ranked seventh amongst the most fatal of diseases. A suitable vaccine was not developed until well into the twentieth century.

## Poliomyelitis

Poliomyelitis, better known by its shortened name of polio, was a highly infectious disease spread by human contact – and it primarily affected children. Polio infected the spinal cord and then the brain which resulted in limb paralysis. The polio virus initially entered the body via the mouth and multiplied.

It is thought that polio may have existed amongst the ancient Egyptians but there were few early epidemics of the disease. Due to the scarceness of a serious illness, the disease was not seen by the medical profession as a threat until the late eighteenth century. In 1789 Michael Underwood, a London paediatrician, published a description of *paralytic disease of infants* and during the nineteenth century, small numbers of polio outbreaks were reported in the medical journals when the disease was referred to as *a debility of the lower extremities.*

Polio, as an epidemic disease, existed mainly in the industrial areas of England, indirectly because of significant improvements in hygiene and public health. Protection from polio became generational because mothers who had survived polio passed on immunity to their babies. The first stage of the polio infection stayed in the digestive system and throat and did not reach the central nervous system. Most babies with maternal immunity suffered only mild flu-like symptoms. Exposure to the first stage also gave them their own long-term immunity.

Throughout the nineteenth century, the lack of detailed knowledge about polio gave rise to many different descriptions, some of which were used to describe causes of death on certificates and occasionally in parish register burial entries. A selection of the entries appears here:

- dental paralysis
- infantile spinal paralysis
- essential paralysis of children
- regressive paralysis
- myelitis of the anterior horns
- paralysis of the morning.

## Dropsy
Known medically as oedema, dropsy was a term to describe the swelling of soft tissue caused by accumulation of excessive amounts of fluid in the body. It was usually associated with or caused by kidney disease or congestive heart failure.

Dropsy was commonly treated using flowers and herbs such as foxglove or digitalis. Dropsy or oedema was usually secondary to the main cause of death but is frequently seen and used as the cause of death on early death certificates.

# CHAPTER 5

# VICTORIAN MEDICINES AND REMEDIES

For most Victorians life was hard with many living below the poverty line, so much so, that drugs and medicines became a vital commodity. Most Victorians could obtain a wide range of drugs over the counter without a prescription at a pharmacy; there was no consultancy charge whereas doctors had to be paid for consultations.

Drug-taking played a huge role in Victorian culture and it was fully endorsed and even encouraged by the drug industries of the day, particularly those involved in tobacco, tea, coffee and alcohol manufacture. The nineteenth century was an important period of development for drugs in terms of effectiveness and range. The Victorians regularly used alcohol, opium and cannabis, and following the popularity of the hypodermic needle, from the 1840s onwards they also used morphine and heroin. The Victorian era brought about drug controls, passed legislation to regulate the trade and introduced steps to control addiction to these substances.

The Victorian pharmacy was recognised as an establishment which improved the healthcare of the population for the very first time, allowing the working class in particular to obtain cures and remedies for numerous illnesses and ailments. The establishment of a pharmacy in main shopping streets was ground breaking. The pharmacies stocked ready-made patent and proprietary medicines, as well as their own homemade remedies; they also sold the raw ingredients which could be used for homemade remedies including laudanum used to treat dysentery, *chlorodyne* for the common cold and coughs and camphorated tincture of opium for respiratory problems and asthma.

The walls and shelves in the pharmacy would have many wooden drawers, bottles and boxes containing liquids and powders, all labelled with Latin names. Pharmacists prepared some medicines by weighing out and mixing different ingredients in accordance with the formulae found in the pharmacopeia of the day. The nineteenth-century pharmacopoeia was fairly mundane. Many Victorians were taking new and frequently illegal drugs to treat common ailments such as coughs or colds and toothache.

Both doctors and pharmacists were continually making discoveries which changed the world of medicine. In the early Victorian period, medicine was generally based on established beliefs with herbalists still playing an important role in helping the doctors and pharmacists with information about the remedial properties of herbs and plants. Their knowledge of where these species could be sourced was invaluable. There were a number of common cures used by Victorian pharmacists but there was a grey area between quack remedies and accepted and proven pharmaceutical remedies.

A few facts about some of the accepted remedies of the time now follow.

## Leeches
Many Victorians still believed that an imbalance of 'humours' was responsible for their illness. The main body fluid was blood and they believed that if bleeding occurred, it was because the body had too much blood and this caused many illnesses. So leeches would be used to suck the blood out of the body. Leeches were usually applied under medical supervision but were also available from the local pharmacies for self-medication.

## Plasters
Wax-based leather-strip plasters were used to extract infection from the body. Ingredients such as lead, opium or frankincense – all supposedly

good for clearing infections – would be spread onto the plasters which would be formed into different shapes to be placed on various parts of their body. Again they would supposedly draw out excessive humours which were understood to cause pain or illness. Chest plasters were generally large and frequently used to treat someone with a cough. The plaster would have been left in place for several days and as it was wax-based, the melted wax would become messy and invariably result in other ailments. *Allcock's Porous Plaster* contained a potent mixture including lead oxide and was used to treat coughs and colds by being stuck to the chest providing a warm sensation radiating through their skin.

## Everlasting pills

The Victorians believed that the aim of purging the body of unwanted fluids required a special drug, so the *everlasting pill* was invented. This was very small and made of antimony, a silver-white, poisonous metal. Swallowing the small pills would result in severe vomiting and diarrhoea, supposedly providing a healthy internal cleanse of the body. The pill could be used time and time again – hence its name! After taking a pill, faeces of the patient would be examined in order to retrieve the pill, which was then washed and reused! After a wash, it would be available for further use, usually within the same family but often by more than one generation. (You couldn't make it up, could you?)

## Quack remedies

The word quack is derived from the Dutch language *quacken* meaning *to prattle on about something*. Today our dictionaries define a quack as *an unqualified person who dishonestly claims to have medical knowledge*. Sometimes, quacks were referred to as medical dissenters; but basically, they were medical fraudsters!

The topic of people who practised the arts of quack medicine was discussed at length in volume one; a quack can be briefly summarised as a person usually of good, excellent manners and fine dress so they looked the part. They were neat and tidy – but very slick salesmen! Quacks had to be good talkers, charismatic and believable, especially when they manned their temporary stalls in the marketplaces where they cajoled and persuaded their gullible customers with their convincing sales patter that their products were literally miraculous and could heal … well, just about everything! For example, if the contents of a vial or packet gave off an unusual smell and if it had a suitable *cures all* descriptive label, then it would sell well.

*Quacks at work. A patient sits helplessly in a chair while proponents of different medicines brawl with each other, overturning tables and chairs*

Since health was a high priority for most Victorians, they would almost automatically trust anything that claimed to make them feel better; they were completely taken in by the extreme and outlandish claims made by quacks about the miracle powers of the pills, potions and powders they sold, so quack medicine was extremely popular and well-established. Most of the Victorian population were unable to afford proper medical treatment or care; those living in rural areas still relied heavily on herbal and ritual remedies so the occasional visit from a travelling quack often meant something new could be tried.

But there is no doubt there were many disadvantages and even dangers associated with quack remedies, many of which simply didn't work because they were dangerously addictive and could cause long-term damage to users. The exploitation of Victorian medical ignorance was rife; many of the medicines sold made matters worse because many so-called cures contained poisons to a varying degree:

- people suffering weight loss were told to digest tapeworms
- crying babies were drugged with opioids to make them sleep
- babies were given teething powders containing arsenic
- heroin was used in children's cough medicine
- opium and tobacco were sold as cures for asthma
- morphine was prescribed for menstrual cramps.

Fortunately these quack treatments were eventually wiped out from around 1860 when the Adulteration of Food and Drink Act was passed but it did not have immediate effect. Prior to the legislation, the frequency of epidemics was evident, probably caused in part by the cheap poisons and addictive drugs sold by the quacks.

Interestingly, one of the most well-known early tonics, originally claiming to be a "cure-all" for most diseases, was *Coca Cola*, first produced in 1886. Initially it was high in caffeine and cocaine making it highly addictive. *Coca Cola* was marketed as a non-alcoholic drink and was a popular beverage especially in the temperance movement. The cocaine element was permanently removed from the drink in 1904. It was not until the Dangerous Drugs Act of 1920 that drugs containing opium, heroin, cocaine and morphine could no longer be sold over the counter.

## Further examples of quack remedies

- *Anti-asthma cigarettes.* In the Victorian period cigarettes were considered a health benefit. Asthmatics would inhale smoke hoping to rid themselves of the condition. *Cigares de Joy* became a mainstream treatment for winter coughs. In 1875 the *Medical Times and Gazette* described them as *very useful little agents*. However, they contained *stramonium*, a herbal medicine which caused hallucinations.

- *Chloroform for hiccups.* Victorians were advised to inhale chloroform to rid them of hiccups, but it actually damaged vital organs and the nervous system.

- *Cocaine for toothache.* Cocaine was widely recommended as an anaesthetic for toothache. Dentists also used cocaine during treatment which in many cases led to addiction.

- *Strychnine for fatigue.* People used strychnine pills to stay alert. A relatively small dose could kill and/or cause a rapid heart rate, unconsciousness and cold sweats.

- *Pectoral Balsam of Honey.* This was a patent but ineffective medicine for coughs, colds, asthmas and consumptions containing honey, *tolu balsam* and opium.

- *Frog in your throat lozenge.* This cough lozenge launched in 1894 used novel marketing by offering retail chemists cash prizes for the best frog-related window display. Chemists took up the idea and used elaborate displays to seduce the public. This was a quack remedy that at best soothed the throat but did not cure the cough.

- *Tricosian powder.* This was a product used for hiding grey hair and whiskers by colouring them black or brown. It was said to assist with hair growth and to improve its texture. It was not able to be removed from skin or clothes and often caused real embarrassment to any user.

## Patent medicines

The development of industrial factories and the railways in the nineteenth century encouraged people to move; many migrated from rural areas to the towns and cities where work was more plentiful and better paid. The increasing standards of education meant that more people could read, newspapers were popular and all sorts of adverts were now being noticed. People were also willing to spend money on new medicinal remedies and include them in their home medical chests.

One of the most well-known Victorian patent medicines was *Holloway's Universal Medicine.* The clue is in the name … it was a universal product which would cure everything! No wonder it was appealing. The history of how Thomas Holloway's Universal Family Ointment and Pills came about is interesting and can be seen in appendix 3.

## Phrenology

The definition of phrenology is the *detailed study of the shape and size of the cranium as a supposed indication of character and mental abilities*. It was all to do with feeling the bumps and dips on a person's head! The Victorians were obsessed with the function of the body and phrenology was a way that the slick-talking quacks explained the personality and the ailments associated with mental illness; even some physicians did the same. Whether people viewed this as science or a quack curiosity depended to some extent on social class but nearly everyone considered phrenology as having some substance. It became particularly popular amongst the young and the wealthy and advocated many of the opinions and prejudices of the age.

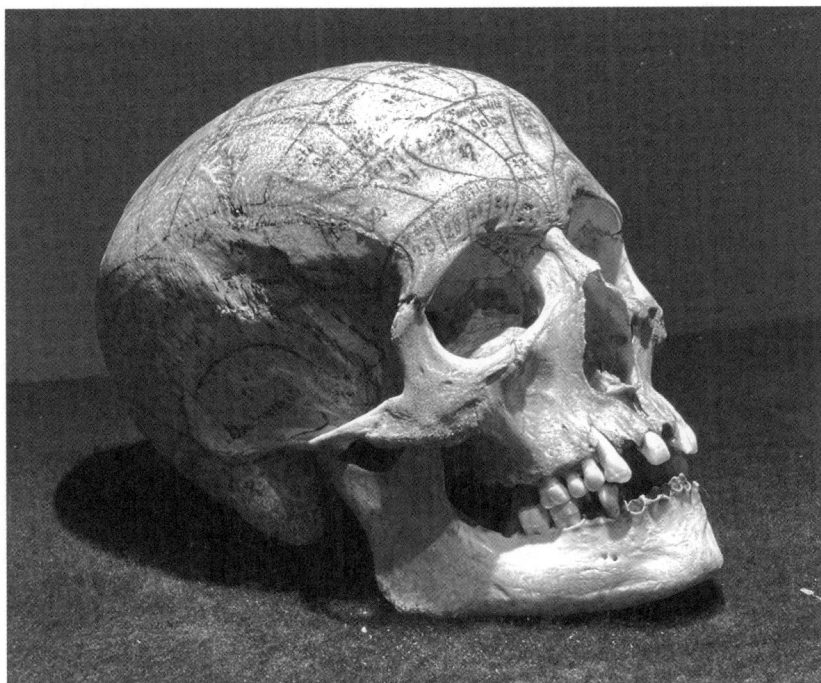

*Phrenology*

The theory behind phrenology was that the brain was made up of twenty-seven organs and it was by measuring or feeling for these organs and noting any irregularities that enabled medics to deduce a person's character. Phrenology was used in the diagnosis of various mental conditions; even the Metropolitan Police tried it in an attempt to try and prevent criminals from re-offending. A criminal's phrenological results were kept on file together with other information. It was also part of the standard treatment of mental conditions in Broadmoor Criminal Lunatic Asylum and in many local asylums.

## Mrs Beeton's *Book of Household Management*

You may wonder what this book has to do with medical treatments but Mrs Beeton's book could be regarded as the householder's bible! It was used universally by most households during the Victorian period and whilst it is perhaps most associated with food and household preparations, it includes a large section on health and the treatment of common ailments and disease.

The heading to that section reads *How to keep Well, Infectious and Contagious Diseases, Non-Infectious Diseases and their Remedies, Common Complaints and their Remedies and What to do in Cases of Accident or Sudden Illness*. In her introduction she states the following:

> *Health of body and mind is a blessing of such inestimable value and is so obviously one of the greatest sources of earthly happiness, that the efforts of all wise persons should be directed towards its attainment. As disease is simply a departure from perfect health, our earliest attention should be given to the chief agents which produce any disturbance of, or departure from, absolute health, so that we may be the more able to combat them successfully. The innumerable external influences which disturb the natural condition of our organs, or the balance of the functions which they perform, as, for example, excess or privation of the air we breathe, the water we drink, the food we eat; variations in the direction of the superabundance or deficiency of the light, heat, and electricity which modify the nutrition of our bodies: all these are*

*among the prime factors in the disturbance of human health, and as
such demand our serious consideration.*

In addition to sections on how to maintain personal hygiene and how
important sleep is, she then proceeds to outline information on the symptoms, causes, complications and treatment of infections and the dangers
of contagion; in particular she alludes to smallpox, scarlet fever, measles,
mumps, rickets, whooping cough, ringworm, typhoid and cholera. She also
mentions asthma, bronchitis, gastric ulcer, piles, lumbago, rheumatism and
many other common but milder complaints. Details are also given on what
to do the event of a sudden illness or accident. So this is why her book
became the acceptable home-doctor book of its day.

Of course, much of Mrs Beeton's book was about food with instructions on
how to buy, store, cook and preserve food. But she also helpfully included
recipes for making poultices, ointments and liniments for medical use.
Many of her recipes for ointments emphasised the continued traditional
use of herbs and plants. Here is an example of how to make an ointment
to soothe chapped hands.

*Ingredients – 1oz of bitter almonds, oil of sweet almonds, the yolk of
1 egg, a little tincture of benzoin and 10 drops of oil of caraway.*

*Mode – Blanch the almonds, beat them to a paste by working in
gradually the oil of sweet almonds and the egg, then add the benzoin
and oil of caraway, and beat till the ointment is of the consistency of
thick cream. Before going to bed, the hands should be well washed
with soap and warm soft water, thoroughly dried with a soft cloth
and the ointment then rubbed well into them. It is desirable to keep
the hands covered with a pair of soft kid gloves while the ointment is
upon them.*

She lists domestic medicines and what they should be used for including
substances like alum, Epsom salts, magnesia, spirits of camphor and so
on. There is even a chapter in the book devoted solely to homeopathic
medicine.

It is not surprising, therefore, that many families kept a comprehensive medicine chest and practised self-medication as well as visiting the
pharmacy to obtain drugs which were readily available over the counter
– including many patent medicines, some of which were questionable, as
we have seen!

# CHAPTER 6

# THE HEALTH CONSEQUENCES OF VICTORIAN LIFE

The Victorian era was known as the age of industry and innovation. To the householder this meant new and different things coming onto the market all the time. Virtually every Victorian was influenced by *keeping up with the Jones's*, so they followed the trends as they happened.

Accidents are caused by many different things and they can be small mishaps like a broken vase or big calamities or even tragedies such as illnesses; but many of these were caused by their style and conditions of living. Even today, people have accidents in the home due to incorrect use of microwave ovens and other appliances. So it was in Victorian times – the simplest objects could turn out to be death-defying!

## Wallpaper

The Victorian's choice in home décor demanded wallpaper in every room. It was the new big thing!! And it was called Paris Green wallpaper because it included a green pigment. This pigment was cheap to produce and was used in everything from clothes to wallpaper.

After the coloured wallpaper started to be mass-produced, people suddenly began to fall mysteriously ill and it was subsequently discovered that one of the ingredients of the Paris Green pigment was arsenic! This meant that all Victorians were decorating their houses with a poisonous chemical.

Humidity in the rooms caused the arsenic in the wallpaper to disperse into the air; people would therefore unknowingly inhale the fumes which affected the respiratory system. Simply touching the wallpaper was also unsafe and if infants chewed or licked it, this sometimes made them so ill they died. As more and more people fell ill and many subsequently died, doctors began to link the deaths to arsenic which was in the Paris Green wallpaper and used in other commercial and household dyes. Although the medical profession made the public aware of the dangers, it was too late for some and cost many lives.

## Staircases

As the population grew, particularly in towns and cities, this meant more houses were needed. With the increase in the building of houses, one area of design that was often overlooked was the staircase. Most were made too narrow or too steep; sometimes steps were very irregular and many staircases were poorly constructed and actually insecure and unsafe. Servants' staircases were considered to be particularly dangerous. Add in the weight of carrying trays or the complication of long skirts, and the stairs could cause many serious injuries and fatalities.

## Laudanum

Laudanum, known as the *aspirin of the nineteenth century*, was a form of opium diluted in alcohol and it was found in virtually every Victorian medicine cabinet. Laudanum was sold by apothecaries and chemists; several other addictive drugs derived from cocaine were also available over the counter as normal remedies that people could buy. It is difficult to determine how many people died of opiate poisoning during the Victorian era because the effects of addiction rarely appeared as a cause of death on certificates.

It was used as a popular painkiller and relaxant, recommended for all sorts of ailments including coughs, rheumatism, *women's troubles* and as a tranquilliser for babies and children. Even nineteenth-century cough mixture included drops of laudanum.

Its use was unregulated, highly addictive and had a long-term debilitating effect and often causing death. Those addicted to laudanum suffered from periods of euphoria usually followed by periods of depression, together with restlessness and sometimes slurred speech. They also suffered withdrawal symptoms including cramp, nausea and diarrhoea but it was not until the early twentieth century that it was recognised as addictive.

At the end of the nineteenth century, the introduction of aspirin as a pain reliever significantly reduced any reliance on opium-based patent medicines. The Victorians had until then relied on other opium-based patent medicines which were available without prescription. These included:

- Batley's Sedative Solution
- Dover's Powder
- Dalby's Carminative
- Kendal Black Drop
- McMunn's Elixir
- Mother Bailey's Quieting Syrup.

## Opium

Since 1756 when Britain captured Calcutta, the cultivation of poppies for opium formed an important part of the East India Company's business. Opium therefore played an important part in Victorian life and preparations were sold freely in towns and most rural markets making the consumption of opium popular.

Areas such as London's docklands and the East End were well-known locations for opium dens as indeed were some of the other port cities around Britain. In the mid-1800s, a small Chinese community settled in the slums of Limehouse Reach, part of London's docklands, an area which also boasted seedy backstreet pubs and brothels. The opium dens catered for seamen who became addicted to the drug while overseas.

*Opium dens typical of those frequented by sailors in East London*

The India-China opium trade was very important to the British economy. Britain had fought two opium wars in the mid-nineteenth century because of the immense profits to be made in the trading of opium. Companies exporting opium from India to China sold it to fund shipments of tea to the extent that in 1839, the first of two opium wars broke out between Britain and China over the trade. A potted history of these two wars can be found at appendix 5.

Many of the opium-based preparations were targeted at women, marketed as *women's friends* and widely prescribed by doctors for pain relief during menstruation and childbirth. They were also common for treatments of the fashionable *vapours* including hysteria and fainting fits. Children were also given opiates to keep them quiet and were often spoon-fed *Godfrey's Cordial* which was referred to as *mother's friend*. It was a mixture of water, treacle and opium and used in the treatment for colic and hiccups amongst other things. Overuse of Godfrey's Cordial resulted in either severe illness or death among infants and young children.

The Pharmacy Act of 1868 attempted to control the sale and supply of opium-based preparations as they could only be sold by registered chemists but such controls were largely ineffective as they did not control the amounts that could be sold. The Victorian attitude to opium was inconsistent because middle and upper classes regarded the heavy use of laudanum among the lower classes as misuse, but they still used their own opiates which they regarded as a habit and not misuse.

Victorian centres of opium-smoking is based on the fact that in the mid-1880s Chinatowns started to appear in London and Liverpool with grocery stores, eating houses, meeting places and Chinese street names particularly around London docks. In 1891, eighty per cent of those born in China and living in London were seamen.

## Baby bottles

Feeding babies from a bottle was nothing new in Victorian times but a special glass bottle fitted with rubber tubing and a teat was a Victorian innovation. The bottles were mass-produced after prominent advertising campaigns and were branded as *The Little Cherub*. If a child could feed itself, it was a source of great pride to mothers. The bottles were extremely popular with mothers but frequently had deadly consequences.

The rubber tubing was impossible to clean because of the way it was designed. Filling the bottle with warm milk actually created a breeding ground for bacteria. Mrs Beeton, the household guru of the day, advocated in 1861 that it was not necessary to wash the bottles for a week or two. For many babies the consequences were fatal and the bottles became known as *murder bottles*.

## Toilets

Although toilets had been around for centuries, the bathroom was very much a Victorian innovation. The idea of a dedicated room for personal hygiene is a modern evolution; most houses built before the turn of the twentieth century didn't have bathrooms and householders relied on the outside privy which was often shared by many families.

Who would have thought that toilets and baths were a health hazard? But when they were first invented, they were indeed often dangerous to health! There were a number of cases of people being scalded in the bath and a few cases of death by lavatories spontaneously exploding! Flammable gases such as methane and hydrogen sulphide, stemming from human waste, frequently built up in the old sewers and leaked back into the bath-rooms, including indoor toilets, and these fumes could be ignited by a candle flame.

Thomas Crapper is credited inventing the flushing toilet, with his valve-and-siphon design patented in 1891 after which his company manufactured water closets. However, in the late eighteenth and early nineteenth century, better sewage systems were being designed so patents were also granted for several different types of WC valves – but most suffered from inadequate flushing actions. The wall-mounted cistern that became popular in the 1870s vastly improved the situation because it provided a large volume of water under more pressure. The pans presented a problem because their traps didn't get rid of waste; but more importantly they were ineffective at keeping sewer gases out of the building. At first these bowls were made of earthenware and glazed sometimes with elaborate designs.

## Tallow candles

In the nineteenth century most candles were made from tallow or beeswax. Tallow burned with a sooty flame and had a pungent smell. In 1810 a method was discovered which involved separating tallow and adding an ingredient which made high-quality candles. The craze for these *com-pound candles* peaked around 1835 and 1836. However, a garlic-type odour emanating from the melted wax caused concern because the smell was similar to arsenic which was addictive and poisonous. The *Lancet* described the candles as *corpse candles* because of their deadly vapour. They were responsible for the deaths of many before gas lighting existed, although such a cause may not have been recorded on the death certificate.

## Collars, cuffs and billiard balls

In 1856 English chemist Alexander Parkes received the first of several patents on a plastic known as *Parkesine*. This was made by dissolving highly flammable nitrocellulose in solvents such as alcohol or wood naphtha and mixing in various plasticisers. This was the first synthetic plastic material, developed in the 1860s and 1870s.

These early plastics became very desirable because they allowed everything from brooches and hair combs to collars, cuffs and billiard balls to be made cheaply. Unfortunately, it was also highly flammable and as it degraded or wore down, it could self-ignite and explode on impact. It is known to have caused many serious injuries and burns and did result in some fatalities particularly from being burned during a game of billiards.

## Gas lighting

For years, most people had relied on candles and firelight for heat and light in their homes, but improvements in science and engineering meant that a controllable source of light to society was now available. The advantages were life-changing to some. Houses, factories, street lights and shops could now be illuminated on a scale which was, until then, inconceivable.

Gas lighting was introduced into the Victorian home meaning that rooms were illuminated much better than the light previously provided by candles or night lights. But the improvement also brought its dangers. The gas used to fuel the lights was odourless and installations were prone to leakage. Therefore unsuspecting occupants of any gas-lit room could become unconscious and may have eventually died. Regardless of the risk, homes all over England were equipped with gas lighting. Coal gas included a lethal combination of hydrogen, methane, carbon monoxide and sulphur. Not only was this highly flammable but the residents of a house could have suffered carbon monoxide suffocation where there was poor ventilation.

The Victorians appreciated scientific progress and there were few regulations on these new products. It was also the era of mass advertising which created a rather lax easy-going society which resulted in many accidents. Sometimes malicious behaviour also cost people their lives. Low gas pressure was a frequent problem caused by fractures in pipes and joints due to poor workmanship, an accident or even sabotage. There was a significant increase in reports of fires, explosions and suffocations resulting in fatalities, often of whole families.

## Contaminated foods

During the Victorian era industrialisation and mass production of foods led to a greater variety of manufactured food products. Commercial organisations were only interested in making profits so many food manufacturers would add any old ingredients which were cheap, gave more substance and bulk to the product yet created the impression that their products were of high quality. Nearly everything was adulterated in some form or other from bread and mustard to blended tea; the problem was these additives often contained poisonous elements such as lead for colouring.

The adulteration of foods was common and dangerous. Here are some of the consequences:

- it caused malnutrition
- it caused deadly diseases and sometimes death
- additives were frequently highly toxic
- chalk, bone meal and alum added to bread
- plaster of Paris, bean powder and iron sulphate added to bread
- borax added to milk
- sloe, hawthorn and other plants added to tea
- sand, rice, gypsum and sulphates of lime added to tea.

Bread was an essential part of the Victorian diet particularly for the poor; it was substantial, filling, readily available and inexpensive. Few people had ovens so they relied on the village baker who would carry out every part of the process including the milling, baking and selling of bread. But these occupations gradually became independent; the miller sold his flour to the baker, who in turn sold his bread to the shopkeeper.

It was common for traders to do all they could to increase their profit margins, so it was not surprising that many products were mixed with cheaper substances. Traders also added ingredients to improve the look or taste of a product. Brown bread became unfashionable and so alum was used to whiten the flour. Alum was toxic having been derived from aluminium and it proved particularly deadly for children as it caused diarrhoea, which led to dehydration and often death.

PUNCH, OR THE LONDON CHARIVARI.—November 20, 1858.

THE GREAT LOZENGE-MAKER.
A Hint to Paterfamilias.

*Death portrayed as a lethal confectioner making up sweets using
arsenic and plaster of Paris as ingredients representing the toxic
adulteration of sweets in the 1858 Bradford Sweets Poisoning*

Before pasteurization, milk carried serious health risks; it could give rise to tuberculosis which could be fatal. Milk was then made even more deadly when borax was added to remove any sour flavour; rather than improve the taste of sour milk, Victorians believed borax actually purified the milk! In fact, borax had similar properties to alum – it was harmful to children, caused chronic diarrhoea and serious illness or even death. It also caused skin problems which inevitably caused more infection.

The deregulation of the beer industry in the 1830s meant that anyone could set up a beerhouse and it was common for brewers to not only water down the ale but also add chemicals to boost its head and flavour. Many people regularly drank beer because of poor water quality so the substitutions had a big impact on health over a prolonged period.

The new commercial food producers probably thought they were on to a good thing; a handful or two of alum or chalk to bread wouldn't do much harm, would it? The brewer probably thought the same ... the people would still drink his ale despite it being a bit weak and the ruthless tea blender wouldn't think twice about adding any old cheap dried leaves to his tea – even some chemicals like Prussian blue which made it look posh and expensive! These processes became routine from the mid-nineteenth century; the 1840s and the 1850s appeared to be the peak times for food adulteration.

Since there was a growing awareness of the scale of food adulteration, eventually the first food standards were introduced in the 1860s and this change gathered momentum as the century progressed. Until this point, no one had really known about or fully understood the risks associated with consuming adulterated food. The consequences in some cases were fatal.

## Cleaning products

Once the Victorians became aware of how diseases were transmitted through microscopic germs in the air carried by flies and other insects, they became obsessed with the fashion of cleanliness. Many different types of cleaning products and poisons became readily available as household cleaning items, but if these were misused there were severe consequences including death. For example, in many cases of suicide investigated by the coroners and police, it was found that cleaning materials containing poison had been used to end life.

Victorians of all classes linked cleanliness to respectability, hence the proverb *cleanliness was next to Godliness* and this intensified their pre-occupation with tackling germs. Most chemical cleaning products were extensively marketed, advertised, and proved highly effective. The products were contained in bottles and packages but ... unfortunately they were frequently indistinguishable from other household products. For example, caustic soda used for cleaning and baking powder used in cooking were packaged in almost identically labelled and shaped boxes so were easily mistaken for each other. This led to severe consequences indeed because the cleaning products contained highly toxic ingredients such as carbolic acid. People were poisoned and some even died. Therefore, the Pharmacy Act 1902 made it illegal for bottles of dangerous chemicals to be similar in shape to ordinary liquids.

## Reports of the Medical Officer of Health

Most family historians are keen to place their ancestral families in their contemporary environment as that helps understand the influences which affected their individual lives. The general health of our ancestors really depended upon where they worked and lived – were their surroundings healthy or not? The medical officers were influential in many of the nineteenth-century reforms that took place. Sanitation and public health were a major concern in Victorian Britain as any improvements would have enhanced the lives of our ancestors and their families.

There was a population explosion in Victorian times, which in itself was problematic, but in addition, problems were created due to people moving from rural areas to urban towns and cities, mainly to look for work. New expanding towns as well as the old towns all had narrow streets and high-density housing, so the health and social problems increased. Unfortunately, basic public health fell short of what was needed and some local authorities were unable to provide an adequate water supply, sanitation and street cleaning.

Medical Officers of Health were ultimately responsible for the health of the community. They were mostly qualified medical practitioners but were not directly concerned with individual health. However, their responsibility for the community meant that the lives of all our ancestors would be influenced for the better by any improvements the authorities made.

Medical Officers sent quarterly reports to central government. Although mainly statistical, when used in conjunction with valuable information contained in the census, the government was able to identify future needs of a community; they could consider such elements as housing, schools and hospital provision. One of the biggest challenges facing a medical officer was how to overcome overcrowded living conditions and how to reduce infectious diseases within a community.

A primary role of the medical officer was to provide isolation and fever hospitals; they also had the powers to close schools in an epidemic. The medical officers were assisted by health visitors and sanitary inspectors who were part of the team and they all contributed to the quarterly reports and processes to improve local conditions.

The reports of local medical officers of health are normally deposited in local record offices and many of them have been published. The Wellcome Library in London has an almost complete collection of the reports. These reports provide an insight into the environmental conditions from the late nineteenth century onwards; for family historians, the information on deaths is highly valuable. Most reports categorised deaths by gender and age. The reports also specified the number of deaths from various diseases.

### The new London sewer system
For years the river Thames was called London's open sewer. The old sewer pipes were completely inadequate and useless as they emptied untreated human waste directly into the river. As the population expanded in the city, so did the smell, and this came to a head in a hot July in 1858 – it was called *the Great Stink*! It was clear something had to be done because the city's population suffered many health issues due to this dreadful smell and lack of proper sewers.

So Parliament decided to improve the city's sanitation and sanctioned a new sewerage system which would make a significant difference to London's general health. It also physically transformed riverside areas and the river Thames itself. This new sewage system opened in 1865. New street sewers had been constructed and these connected into a network of main intercepting sewers which took all London's sewage downstream; from there it was pumped into the tidal reaches of Thames so that it could be immediately taken out to sea.

It took time for all this work to be done and unfortunately some residents in the slum areas of East London succumbed to an outbreak of cholera in 1866 because they had not been connected to the system. That outbreak of cholera was the last because by the end of that year, most people's houses had been fully connected to the new sewage system.

Through his investigations into the living conditions of the poor, Edwin Chadwick concluded that elements such as cleaning, drainage and ventilation would improve the health of working people and allow them to be less dependent on the welfare systems of the day. The measures introduced by Chadwick were based on the current medical intelligence. The aim of the later Public Health Act in 1875 was for local authorities to replace the local boards and be responsible for providing clean water, proper drainage and managed sewage disposal.

### Dr John Snow

This gentleman is worthy of mention. Dr John Snow was an epidemiologist whose forte was the incidence, distribution and control of infectious diseases. In 1849 he made the following statement about cholera in London. *Many of the earlier cases this year occurred in persons employed amongst the shipping in the river, and the earliest cases in Wandsworth and Battersea have generally been amongst persons getting water direct from the Thames.*

Having witnessed the earlier outbreaks, he made a breakthrough in understanding the cause of the disease after the third epidemic in 1854 and became convinced that it was caused by water contaminated by raw sewage. That same year, he demonstrated this by mapping cases of the illness to a particular water pump in Soho. That outbreak killed over 740 people in one month – but as soon as the pump in Soho was shut down, the epidemic completely subsided.

In 1868 Snow found that residents in areas where the water companies extracted water from locations where the sewers emptied into the Thames suffered a much higher death rate than those whose water was supplied further upstream who ceased to become seriously ill.

### *Cholera prevention*

Cholera was widespread so the government issued information about taking precautions and also informed the people of recommended remedies. This prevention advice was distributed on large posters through the city – many of our ancestors would have benefitted from the advice. A lengthy extract from one of these widespread posters can be seen at appendix 4.

# CHAPTER 7

# HEREDITARY DISEASES

In Victorian times there were strong traditions based on folklore about how traumatic events encountered by a pregnant woman could affect a child and also how disease and other ailments were passed from generation to generation within the same family. In 1886 the *British Medical Journal* printed an article about a child with a deformed hand; he was the fourth generation in the same family to suffer from the same deformity.

It is likely when researching your family history that you will have discovered some ancestors who married their own cousins. This is known officially as *consanguinity* which is defined as *the act of marrying a biological relative*. Consanguinity is derived from *con* meaning with and *sanguin* meaning blood, and the practice of *keeping it in the family* had been going on for centuries – from the Egyptians or earlier to royal families across for world. In those days, people really believed that marrying a relative would preserve the bloodline and any children surely had to be flawless, genuine and unadulterated.

Some families were lucky and all went well, but other dynasties suffered through the years and subsequent generations suffered from hereditary diseases. In a nutshell, it's all to do with DNA. But they knew nothing of that at the time – it had not even been discovered!

But hereditary diseases are not always genetic. A genetic disease is a gene mutation which can be inherited; some family members may not inherit such a mutation. It could lay dormant thereby skipping generations. DNA studies have indicated that we are still affected by mutations which originated as early as the Black Death. This has been proven recently when teeth from skeletons unearthed from the East Smithfield plague pit in London were analysed.

Conversely, there are many hereditary conditions which are not genetic. Hereditary conditions usually occur in at least three generations of a family. The history of your family's medical past is not just about genes because other factors such as lifestyles, diet and environmental exposures can be shared within your family.

Swiss physiological chemist, Friedrich Miescher, first identified *nuclein* in white blood cells in 1860 but it wasn't until 1943 that scientists realised DNA was genetic; ten years later, the double helix was found – and the rest, as they say, is history. From that date onwards, scientists all over the world have specialised in DNA and experiments and trials are ongoing.

As a result of this, today's family historians have the luxury of doing a DNA test and this side of family history research has grown enormously in recent years; many researchers have been able to identify and find long-lost relatives, proved to be so, by DNA test results. The amount of detailed information on what the DNA tests reveal is extensive and there are hundreds of books being written about this sole topic, so since the scope of this book only goes up to 1950, it would be inappropriate to go into the detailed subject of DNA in these pages.

However, to return to hereditary diseases, here are a few famous historical figures who suffered from diseases which were deemed to be hereditary.

**King Charles II of Spain** was the last Hapsburg King of Spain and had a peculiar long jaw-line which made him drool a lot and apparently he could hardy speak let alone eat! He also had great difficulty walking. He died aged thirty-nine.

**Emperor Ferdinand I of Austria** was born with hydrocephaly in 1793. Many Hapsburgs suffered from this disease. Basically it is water-on-the-brain.

Ferdinand also had the famous Hapsburg long jaw and he suffered from epilepsy.

**Alexei Romanov**, the grandson of Queen Victoria, inherited haemophilia which was also called the *royal disease*. This is a disease where any bump or fall can cause bruising and then severe bleeding which can be fatal. Queen Victoria married Prince Albert and he was her first cousin and this meant that Queen Victoria, who had the blood-clotting disease herself, passed it on to all her children.

**King Tutankhamen** was severely incapacitated. After his tomb was discovered, his mummy was scanned and it revealed that he had a cleft palate, club foot and an elongated skull.

When you have an idle moment, it is well worth browsing the topic on the internet. There appear to be many articles about famous people who have suffered various diseases. We all know that **Beethoven** suffered deafness towards the end of his life and some people believe that **Julius Caesar** had epilepsy. But were they hereditary diseases or not?

The medical definition of disease is *an interruption, cessation, or disorder of a body, system, or organ structure or function*. Causes of disease are defined as follows:

- accumulation of toxic material, for example through poor diet
- incorrect or unbalanced diet
- improper posture
- destructive emotions
- the use of suppressive drugs and vaccines
- use of alcohol, caffeine and tobacco
- environmental hazards – air and water pollution
- occupational hazards
- inherited factors and predispositions
- infections.

To some degree family status and social class was significant. It was considered important to the medical profession to know the beliefs, attitudes and social standing of a family rather than determining what was making the disease a matter of inherited susceptibility and individual lifestyle. Climate and location were also thought to make a difference. Infection which was transmitted by water and air was not generally considered relevant.

Throughout the Victorian era most people felt that the doctor knew best when it came to medical treatment so they hankered after the latest medical and surgical treatments, often overlooking common sense or obvious remedies.

Poorer working-class families were sometimes rebellious and often questioned the systems or were extremely cautious when having to deal with circumstances that were unfamiliar to them. Most of them could not afford medical treatment and some would not trust the system anyway. Many people developed nutritional-based diseases and became alcohol-dependent as well as being frequent victims of accidents.

# CHAPTER 8

# ACCIDENTS AT WORK – FACTORIES, MINES AND CHEMICAL PLANTS

## Overview

During the nineteenth century which was the Victorian era known as the *age of industry and innovation,* many workplaces were dangerous and there are several reasons for this. Mechanisation was present in almost every trade and industry from rural and agricultural businesses to work in factories and on the railways to say nothing of work underground in the mines. Machinery was unprotected and dangerous and many workplace accidents were caused by bosses employing an unskilled or untrained workforce on the new machines. An additional problem from using machines meant that workers were exposed to toxic substances used in some industrial and agricultural processes; there was also continuous noise, poor ventilation and lighting and lots of dust and grit.

The mills and mines were generally crowded and had little, if any, fresh air and ventilation. Work was monotonous and repetitive so there was little stimulation. In factories, machines often broke down; drive belts could snap or become dislodged from the overhead pulley systems and people were working amidst the machinery to keep them running or to carry out maintenance and repairs. Most workers whether in rural locations working on farms or in an artisan trade or in urban areas working in the mines, mills and factories worked ten or twelve hours day with only thirty minutes allowed for a dinner break. And they did this usually for six days each week.

All these factors affected every worker's health; many suffered long-term effects from deafness to respiratory diseases often contributing to an early death. Adequate medical treatment was not usually provided by employers and overseers and employers had little tolerance regarding the debilitating ailments affecting their workers. However, there were exceptions because some philanthropic employers provided housing, medical treatment, schools and other social amenities. A good example of that is Saltaire and Bournville although such centres were few and far between.

Endless accidents happened in the workplace so records of those employees affected include:

- coroners' inquests
- hospital admission and patient records
- records of the Factories and Mines Inspectorate
- railway company accident records for both employees and passengers
- individual company and business records
- Board of Trade records
- provincial and national newspapers
- records of the shipping companies
- court and litigation records.

No industry escaped the risks of accident or injury, but some were more prone to accidents than others. The *Factory System* exploited cheap labour so anyone was employed. The workforce comprised trained skilled workers, unskilled people and women and children. Some skilled workers themselves actually sub-employed unskilled workers to perform the more menial tasks associated with their job; this invariably meant that women and children were employed as machine minders, machine cleaners and so on.

## Child workers

Pauper and orphan children living in workhouses were frequently "apprenticed" to factory owners; these children worked in the textile trade or in the mines, often unsupervised. They worked long shifts and it was not unusual to find children asleep on the job. The children slept in apprentice houses which were attached to the factory. Beds were shared, so as one shift ended the next started and the beds vacated by children about to start the next shift were used for those had finished their shift. These children were actually employed as cheap labour and worked in very dangerous conditions resulting in injuries or even death. There were plenty of children in orphanages and workhouses so there was never a shortage of child labour; those that were killed or injured and unable to work were easily replaced.

Most families expected their children to work from an early age; their perception of safety was negligible. Some children were formally apprenticed but the less fortunate ones worked in mundane jobs on farms or assisted in cottage industries. When other work became available in the new factories, it was natural to use children for work that adults could not or would not do; these were tasks like crawling underneath machinery to clean or maintain them or sitting in coal mines to open and close the ventilation doors. Many children lost fingers in the machinery and some were killed or crushed by the huge machines.

## Working pay and conditions

In many industries working conditions were appalling. For example, in the mines, young trappers, the youngest member of a family (usually no more than five years old) sat in the dark for their whole shift, opening and closing the gates (traps) for the coal trucks to pass through. Young putters pushed tubs and children as young as six carried coal for the hewer who directly employed them. Women hurriers pulled tubs of coal with a chain that went around their middles and between their legs and did so in a state of partial undress.

These days, people would be screaming *Health and Safety*!! There was none of that really until much later. The first factory inspectors were appointed by

King William IV in 1833. Before then, there was little emphasis on regulating safety issues despite the need having existed since the sixteenth century. Health and safety at work evolved over a couple of centuries, originating from political responses to social problems which arose from the upheavals of the Industrial Revolution. The inadequacies of the various Poor Law Acts had done little to help the situation.

During the early Victorian years, manual workers fell into three groups: skilled, semi-skilled and unskilled although it was sometimes difficult to draw a clear distinction between them. Long working hours of twelve to fourteen hours a day were normal and workers were expected to work additional hours at busy times. Workers were often required to clean and maintain their machines during their mealtimes. A typical wage for male workers was about fifteen shillings a week; women and children were paid much less and that's one reason why employers preferred employing women and children.

No industry, urban or rural, escaped the tragedies of accidents and injury. The sad fact is industrialists usually abandoned their workers from the moment that any accident occurred. Workers' wages would be stopped if they were no longer able to work due to an accident, and in most cases no medical treatment was provided. Whatever the extent of any injury, no compensation was provided except for the select few.

## Rules and discipline
Strict rules were put in place by the more ruthless factory owners – and woe betides anyone who broke the rules! Life was harsh in those days and discipline meted out often seemed very unfair and excessive. Children in particular were fair game and had to suffer bizarre acts of punishment; these included hanging iron weights around their necks, hanging children from the roof in baskets, nailing children's ears to the table and dowsing them in water butts. Frequent strapping, beatings and other punishments took place mainly to keep children and young adults awake.

Workers could be subject to a severe system of fines; these were imposed for talking or whistling, leaving the room without permission, or having dirty machines. In some mills employers themselves even craftily tampered with the time-clocks which made workers appear late and so making them subject to fines. The overseers were often required to raise a certain amount from fines every week.

Records show that about forty per cent of accidents treated in local Infirmaries were as a result of factory accidents. Workers' health was adversely affected in many ways and some of their ailments were specific to their occupation. Accidents and conditions too were often specific to the industry.

Every type of employment involves risk of some kind or another and in those days, many of the risks could be held responsible for causing illness, disease or even worse. For example, physicians have long been aware that the inhalation of dust resulted in some sort of damage to the lungs and therefore could lead to serious diseases like tuberculosis, phthisis, bronchitis or asthma.

It is fairly straightforward to discover the most prevalent diseases associated with any given trade and then investigate their probable causes by considering the conditions that workers had to tolerate. Symptoms connected with an occupation may include a cough, hyperventilation and some wasting diseases. However, some diseases suffered by workers may have had no relation to their employment at all.

**Sir John Simon** 1816-1904 was known as a reformer and whose efforts in this field created modern standards of public health service. After working as a surgeon he then entered Parliament and created a medical department to administer public health to supervise the medical profession. This pioneering work resulted in the Sanitary Act of 1866. This Act saw the start of a public health law as well as the beginnings of industrial hygiene. The Public Health Act of 1875 took this further and legislated for a complete sanitary code that stood the test of time for the next 100 years. It was due to the work of Sir John that significant information relating to manufacturing processes and their effects on health were produced by various factory and mining inspectorates and the Children's Employment Commission.

Most indoor industries used monotonous processes; workers were almost attached to their machines as they did the same thing over and over again. There was little interest or stimulation and this led to periods of low concentration which gave rise to accidents and injuries. Outdoor labour had a distinct advantage over indoor employment; fresh air and movement outside allowed for interaction with other workers and was less monotonous.

Sedentary labour existed in many industries; such jobs included clerks, engravers, artists, tailors and milliners. Shopkeepers exerted the bodily exercise needed to perform their jobs although a retail business in a quiet country town or village was different from the same occupation carried out in the metropolis. Working underground with lack of daylight and poor ventilation with hot moist air in the mine gave rise to many respiratory conditions.

## Mill workers

Machines were loud and thundered relentlessly throughout the day. They also had lots of moving parts and textile mills were by far the most dangerous places to work and there were many accidents. Workers who leaned into machinery to carry out adjustments risked losing a finger, hand or having to have a whole limb amputated as a result of crushing; if they became caught in moving belts, they could easily be scalped. Children were particularly susceptible to accidents as they crawled about on the floor in the dust and dirt doing their menial tasks – many were burnt by dripping hot oil and others would get caught in moving machinery which had no safety guards.

There were many illnesses and diseases suffered by textile mill workers. Deafness and acute hearing problems were common due to the noise; chest infections and lung diseases were also common, caused by the damp and humid atmospheric conditions necessary to keep cotton strong. Fatigue was another problem because workers were required to move quickly all the time to feed a continually running machine. Today we would call this repetitive strain injury which could eventually lead to arthritis. Workers were even killed or seriously injured by the machines which were very slow to stop if any worker was caught up in them. Gradually, changes were made by the government and details of various Acts of Parliament and other preventative solutions regarding accidents at work can be seen at appendix 6.

*Child apprentices in textile factory. Apprentice greeting former friend, the workers in rags.*

## Chimney sweeps and climbing boys

People needed warmth in their dwellings, usually by way of fire, and logic tells us fire creates smoke and the smoke has to go somewhere! In Neolithic times, all that was needed was a hole cut in the grass-and-stone-covered roof; take a leap to Tudor times when houses were built, fires were bigger so chimneys were wider and taller. Enter the chimney sweep and his climbing boys – and sometimes girls!

Fires create smoke and soot which also contains creosote and if a chimney goes on fire, it is usually the creosote that is the cause. So chimneys were swept regularly to remove the dangers of fire. In Tudor times, people could be fined three shillings and sixpence for causing a chimney fire!

Chimneys came in all shapes and sizes; many were straight but others had kinks and bends in them which made life difficult. Most chimney sweeps employed climbing boys; some sweeps looked after their working children well while others exploited them ruthlessly. Climbing boys were often illegitimate children sold to the sweep by their mothers when they were five or six years old. The chimney sweeps became their "owners". A climbing boy had to climb from the fireplace up the stack until he came out at the top. As the boys moved up the chimney they removed the soot from the lining using brushes or metal scrapers. Chimney sweeps encouraged the climbing boy to go up the stack by poking and prodding them; some even lit a fire under the climbing boy's feet, which would force him upwards more quickly.

Accidents were common amongst the chimney sweeps' climbing boys. Some chimneys were usually no more than twelve inches in diameter and climbing them was physically painful and dangerous resulting in several medical issues:

- raw skinless patches which developed calluses
- regular falls and many bruises
- broken legs and ankles
- twisted spines

- eye and breathing problem
- chimney sweep cancer caused by irritation of sensitive skin from coal tar.

The masters did not provide washing facilities for their climbing boys but sometimes they washed the skinless patches with salt water before sending the boy up yet another stack! The more ruthless master chimney sweeps often underfed the boys so that they remained thin enough to continue to move up and down the stacks nimbly and quickly. Many climbing boys had outgrown their job by the time they were nine or ten, although some worked until they were around fourteen years old.

Legislation and other reforms are detailed in appendix 7.

## Coal miners

Coal mining has been around for centuries. In earlier years, coal could be exposed near the surface when people were ploughing or digging the ground; these open pits were then exploited by people and the coal collected was sold to artisans who needed it. In the nineteenth century, coal mining expanded as engineers designed shafts to get at coal underground while other industrialists worked and designed pumps and waterwheels to drain mines.

If any proof were needed to show how coal mining took off in the nineteenth century, just look at these numbers: between 1800 and 1850, there were 3,486 mining accidents; from 1850 to 1900 there were 59,580 accidents! Coal was needed for the huge steam engines in factories and industries; it was also used in the iron industry. It took two tons of coal to produce one ton of iron!

The main areas associated with coal mining are Northumberland and Durham, north and south Wales, Yorkshire, the Scottish central belt, Lancashire, Cumbria, east and west Midlands and Kent. Where there was coal, so associated industries developed. If your ancestors lived in or near any of these areas, there is no doubt they will have been employed in some capacity or other in a mining-associated industry. Many rural agricultural workers migrated to work in the industry too. But it was not always coal that was mined; tin, copper, iron ore, and salt were also mined commercially. (More on that later.)

Coal mines were dark and dangerous places to work and those who worked in the mines suffered from various ailments and faced possible death almost every day.

The main threats in a mine were explosions, flooding and the collapse of tunnels and shafts. Safety has always been a top priority. Methane gas in the mines was known as *firedamp* or *minedamp* and was a flammable gas that was prone to exploding spontaneously which often led to accidents. Sir Humphry Davy came to the rescue when he invented his safety lamp, known as the *Davy Lamp*. Basically the holes in the screen surrounding the flame in the lamp prevented any fire igniting the methane round the lamp. The miners and users of the lamp would know if methane was present nearby because the lamp light burned brighter and had a blue tinge to it.

Miners suffered from low oxygen levels, noxious gases, dim lighting and many suffered long-term illnesses caused by the effects of exposure and inhalation of coal dust. Falls, crushing, suffocation and being drawn over a pulley were other dangers they faced working in the mines. Miners worked long hours in difficult conditions and we have already read that women and children also worked in the coal pits along with the men. The children worked as trappers opening and closing gates and women and older children, known as hurries and thrusters, moved huge tubs and trolleys of coal.

Serious accidents had devastating effects on whole communities. There are many reports of mine accidents in local newspapers and in miners' union records. Many printed notices about accidents provide lists of those killed and injured. Mine records also include correspondence from survivors and relatives of the deceased. Parish burial registers list those killed and buried in the local churchyards or cemeteries. There are often pages of entries following on from each other. If your ancestor was a miner, it is well worthwhile checking with the family history society closest to the mine where he worked. Many such societies have carried out research into mining accidents in their areas.

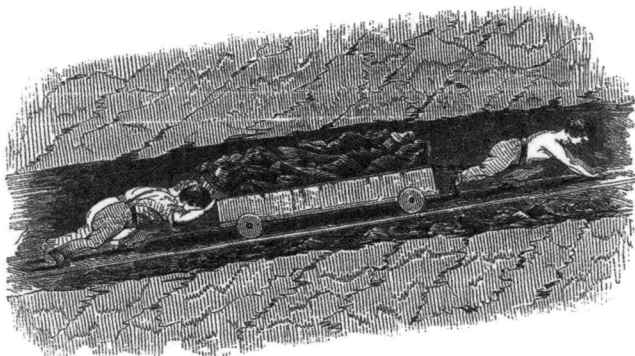

*Children working in mines.*

It became increasingly clear that, as with the textile industries, the government had to step in with legislation and regulations to make coal mines safer places. Further details of parliamentary Acts, inspection reports and accident statistics together with where to find all this information in places like the Coal Mining History Resource Centre, collections of the National Coal Mining Museum and many other sources can all be found in appendix 8.

## Miners' Welfare Fund

The Miners' Welfare Fund was established under the Mining Industry Act 1920 after the Sankey Commission's identification of the appalling living and working conditions of coal miners. It was one of the responsibilities of the Board of Trade and administered by a Miners' Welfare Committee appointed by the Board in January 1921. Its aim was to administer the social well-being, recreation and conditions of living coal miners.

Money for the fund was raised from a levy on coal produced. Between 1920 and 1951, over £30 million was allocated for various purposes including pithead baths, various clubs, institutes and sports fields. Money was also spent on colliery canteens, education and university scholarships, rehabilitation centres for injured miners and research relating to safety in mines. The district committees, in close co-operation with the Mines Department of the Board of Trade, administered the schemes so most surviving records are held locally. The fund existed until the start of World War Two.

## Bevin Boys in the mines

At the start of the Second World War, the government underestimated the value of the younger coal miners without regard to their importance to the mining industry, so many were conscripted into the armed forces. This led to a shortfall of 36,000 mine workers. The government asked for volunteer conscripts to work in the mines but few responded; this manpower shortage was a crisis.

The government then announced that a proportion of conscripts would be redirected to the mines and this is how and why the Bevin Boys were established. Full details about the Bevin Boys can be seen at appendix 9.

## Brickyard and quarry workers

Quarrymen and brickyard workers came from all areas of the country as well as from Ireland. Many Irish workers arrived in England ahead of their families and established themselves before their families finally migrated and joined them.

A quarry was a hive of industrious activity and it was also a dangerous place to work. Quarries had an intricate transport system of tram or narrow-gauge rail lines which transported quarried stone to the cutting and polishing sheds for processing; the heavier blocks of stone were lifted by steam-operated cranes to the work areas where they could be split again into manageable sizes. So with all this activity going on, it is not surprising that accidents took place.

Quarrymen would wear jackets, waistcoats and trousers made of weatherproof moleskin or corduroy. Many also had a knotted neckerchief which was frequently used as a bandage for slight injuries. They also wore iron-shod clogs to protect their feet from injury. The men mostly worked with hand tools with no safety equipment, using hammers, picks, crow bars and sledge hammers to displace the stone from the rock beds. It was hard physical labour.

It was not unusual for clothing to get caught in quarry machinery and workers were often crushed to death or seriously injured by collapsing stone faces or piles of bricks which had not been stacked correctly during manufacture. The constant use of their chisels quickly blunted the tools so frequent visits were made to the quarry blacksmith for him to sharpen them. The blacksmith also made parts for other quarry machines. Burns from brick kilns were common particularly as loading and unloading bricks was a manual process and the kilns were kept going all day every day. Clay and ground subsidence often happened too in the brick-making industry. Accidents on the railway, tramway or sidings when using the narrow-gauge railways to ship stone or clay from quarry to nearby works were almost a daily occurrence.

Other accidents which could occur included the following:

- burns from misfiring of dynamite during stone blasting processes
- injured limbs from falls when climbing ladders on the sides of the quarries
- injuries caused when full wheelbarrows tipped over and fell off the planks

- fatalities were possible if crushed by falling stone
- injuries during shunting operations possibly being crushed between two wagons
- respiratory diseases due to silicosis
- accidents and injuries caused by misuse of hand tools.

There are endless reports in provincial newspapers and in coroners' inquest records of fatalities and serious injuries occurring at quarries. Brickwork accidents were investigated by the Factory Inspectorate.

Prior to the Quarries Act 1894, the only quarries that factory inspectors were responsible for inspecting were those using steam-powered machinery. The Quarries Act 1894 extended the powers of the Metalliferous Mines Regulation Act 1872 to give inspectors the power to enforce the notifying of accidents, undertake prosecutions and to make special rules which led to the establishment of the Quarry Inspectorate whose work affected regulation at open-cast clay pits and quarries.

## Copper and tin miners

Tin, copper and arsenic were found mainly in Cornwall and west Devon so naturally, most of the miners were local to those areas. The legislation which covered coal mines also applied to the tin and copper mines after it was introduced.

The majority of people associate Cornwall with tin mining but when mining in the county was at its peak, it was copper that was being mined and by the early nineteenth century, Cornwall was said to be the largest copper producer in the world. Cornwall had large reserves of copper but by the time the best Cornish copper deposits were exhausted, tin ore had been exposed in the deeper Cornish mines and this resulted in a second mining boom. Deep mining of copper and tin was possible because of sophisticated water-pumping equipment developed by British engineer Richard Trevithick. He developed high-pressure steam engines which were paramount in draining water from the deep mines thereby improving miners' safety as they worked.

The tin industry was much smaller than copper mining so a smaller work-force was needed, but the costs proved to be expensive. Nevertheless, because of the high price of tin worldwide, Cornish tin-mining was very profitable.

In the eighteenth and nineteenth century, millions of tons of tin and copper were produced; the men worked underground in the mines and the women and children worked on the surface. The women were known as *bal maidens; bal* was the Cornish word for a mine. At the height of the tin-mining industry in the late 1830s, around 7,000 children were employed. By 1862 some 50,000 people worked in 340 mines throughout the county.

Miners were responsible for buying their own tools, candles, and dynamite which often meant that they struggled to make a sustainable living because wages were meagre and low. Some mine owners issued six candles a day to the miners but these would barely stay alight. The air was contaminated with dust and deadly fumes from detonated explosives wafted around so some miners chose to extinguish their candles and work in darkness to conserve what little air there was in the mine.

Working conditions were harsh in an extremely cramped and very hot environment. There was little air circulation and temperatures could easily reach 140 degrees Fahrenheit. Mining above or below ground was labour-intensive work; rocks had to be broken up into manageable sizes using small hammers and then loaded onto trolleys and pushed to the crushing machines. Most miners began their employment at the age of twelve years of age but the younger children worked on the surface. All miners, including the women and children, were expected to work a ten-hour day, six days a week.

The industry did not escape disasters. The Levant Mine Disaster of 1919 was one of the worst mining accidents when thirty-one men were killed when an ageing mechanical ladder collapsed. Other accidents were common and there were many reasons for this:

- there were no cages to take the men deep into the mine
- access was by long ladders extending 100 feet
- explosions were caused by unpredictable quills or straw used for fuses
- people tripped when hauling trolleys of coal
- candles and dynamite don't really mix
- rockfalls were common.

These were just some of the hazards of working in a mine. Illnesses caused by the harsh working conditions and the very nature of the job were many:

- falls were common, especially off the long ladders
- broken limbs, twisted ankles and damage to fingers when hit by a hammer
- rockfalls could cause all manner of cut, bruises and injuries
- respiratory diseases such as bronchitis, tuberculosis and phthisis
- silicosis was the biggest fear, a wasting illness caused by mica dust which damaged the lungs
- hearing problems and deafness caused by loud drilling machines.

Despite all these hazards most miners were prepared to risk the possibility of injury or even death because the wages were above average, especially for the underground tin-mine workers. Nevertheless, few miners were fit to work after the age of about forty. Those who worked on the surface generally enjoyed more robust health whilst the miners who spent their lives underground soon showed signs of impeded development.

By the end of the nineteenth century, Cornish tin mining had declined resulting in many mines closing, and by the 1890s, miners were leaving Cornwall to seek employment in other mining areas across the world. This had a huge effect on the county; almost a quarter of a million people left Cornwall. After the decline, the few mines that remained operational began to rely on by-products including arsenic.

Arsenic was present in the tin and copper mines; it was a highly poisonous by-product of tin and was a hazard miners faced on a daily basis. Arsenic workers hardly had any protection from this poisonous substance so fatalities were a frequent occurrence.

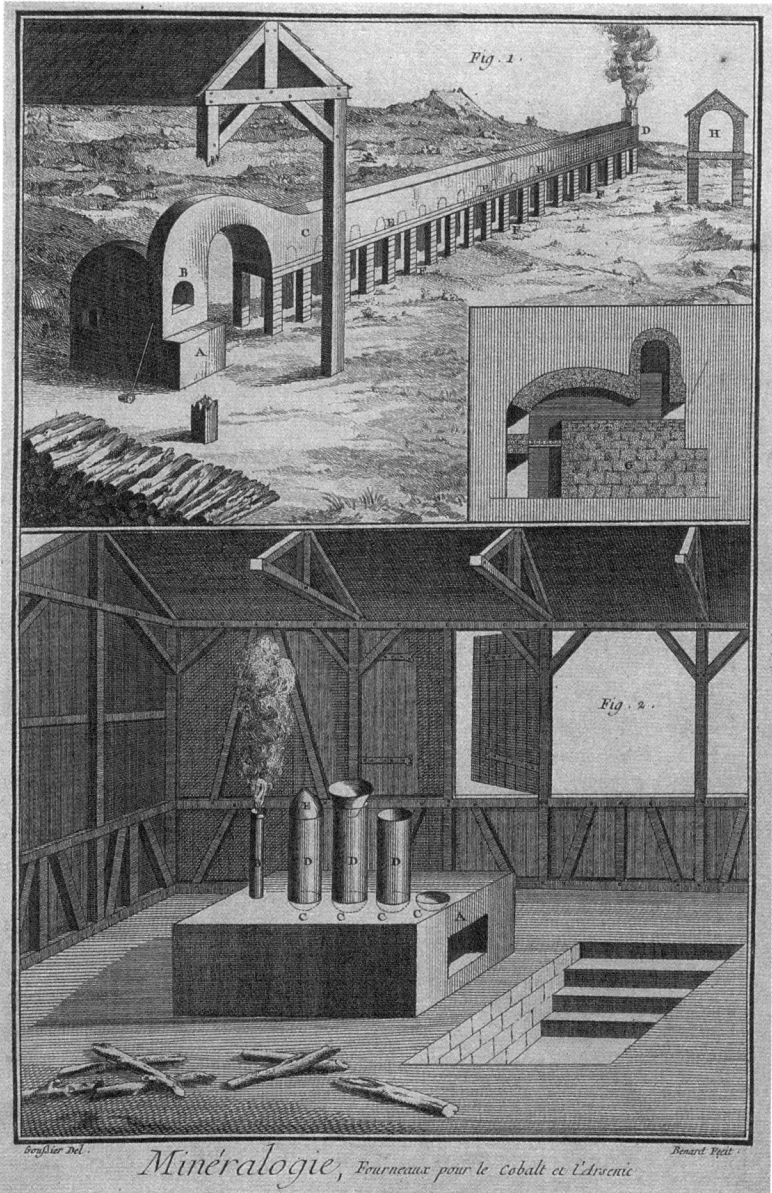

Arsenic furnace used in processing arsenic

The first arsenic was produced at Perranworthal in 1812 and slightly later at Bissoe. There was a ready market because the Lancashire cotton industry used arsenic in the production of pigments and dyes. By the 1880s the arsenic works at Bissoe were producing almost six hundred tons a year of purified arsenic, much of which was sent to the Australia and New Zealand where it was used in sheep dips and glass manufacture. Arsenic was also used as an insecticide and in paint.

Arsenic was produced by heating tin ore to separate the tin. During the process both arsenic and sulphur fumes were emitted. The heating chambers, called *calciners*, would reach temperatures of 600 degrees Centigrade. When these ovens had cooled, workers would scrape the arsenic powder off the walls. Most only wore handkerchiefs over their faces for protection and some smeared their arms with clay to prevent the powder penetrating the skin. Children were left to sweep the arsenic out of the flues – not the most ideal job for kids!!

## Metalworkers and workers in the chemical industries
This group of occupational workers included metal grinders, polishers, toolmakers, cutlers and jewellery makers. These jobs were not as dangerous as mining but without adequate protection these workers were exposed to terrible risks.

Two of the most dangerous metal-working occupations were making files and grinding cutlery. These tasks meant the workers were exposed to many types of metal dust. Over time, cutlers and grinders suffered from respiratory diseases, most of which were progressive; many ended up with ulcerated lungs resulting in death. Paralysis of wrists and hands resulted from repetitive operations.

Workers in chemical factories or in small home workshops were also exposed regularly to toxic fumes from chemicals such as arsenic, lead and mercury; these products were essential to many industrial production processes. Systemic poisoning from exposure to toxic chemicals was inevitable.

Those involved in making lampshades, hats, children's toys such as lead soldiers, matches, fabrics and carpets also suffered from various chemical-induced ailments. Workers who were employed in match pro-duction were affected by white phosphorus, an active ingredient of most matches from the 1840s to the 1910s.

Phossy jaw, medically known as *phosphorus necrosis* of the jaw, was an occupational disease most commonly seen in workers in the match-mak-ing industry. It was caused by vapour from the white phosphorus which affected the bones of the jaw. Sufferers had painful toothache and swelling of the gums spreading progressively to all their teeth and the jawbone. Over time, tooth loss and recurrent abscesses were common leading to necrosis (loss of cells and tissue or blood supply) of the jaw within about six months. The lower jaw was more commonly affected than the upper jaw and affected bones actually glowed when it was dark. In severe cases the condition also affected the brain with some people suffering seizures. Surgical removal of the afflicted jaw bones could be undertaken otherwise death from organ failure would often result. The disease was extremely painful and disfiguring with dying bone tissue rotting away leaving a foul-smelling discharge. Removal of the jaw bone also affected a sufferer's ability to eat, leading to other conditions including malnutrition.

It was the serious concern over contracting phossy jaw that contributed to the London Match-girls' Strike of 1888 at Bryant and May, but their pro-tests and the strike did not stop the use of white phosphorus. When the Salvation Army opened a match-making factory in 1891, their manufactur-ing processes used red phosphorus which was deemed to be much safer. Interestingly, workers employed as clerks and office workers within a match factory environment were almost as badly affected by phossy jaw as the production workers.

# CHAPTER 9

# ACCIDENTS AT WORK –
# LAND AND SEA, ROAD AND RAIL

## Rural workers

Initially, one would presume that working in the countryside was far safer than being employed in the industrial world or in the mines. But people involved in rural industries were equally prone to accidents and injuries. However, few workers were affected by respiratory diseases as most of their work was in the fresh air.

Agricultural labourers suffered many accidents particularly after mechanisation because there was little safety protection. These are some of the sort of accidents that could happen:

- loss or injury to limbs from belts snapping on threshing machines
- stabbing from agricultural tools
- feet could be sliced off by misuse of a plough
- injuries resulting from animals out of control or bolting horses
- respiratory ailments from working with animal skins and hides
- inhalation of insecticides
- hand-threshers suffered respiratory problems from inhaled grain dust and chaff.

Workers and operatives of the wooden post mills were also prone to accidents. Wooden post mills were unpredictable and vulnerable to the effects of the weather. As a result of storms, some were blown over completely so anyone inside them at the time was unlikely to escape broken bones or being injured or stabbed by equipment. Records show that at least one miller was killed by being trapped under a heavy millstone.

People who attended shooting parties in the countryside were prone to accidents. In fact anyone who handled a gun was putting people at risk. Guns were often used to scare the birds off the fields and crops. Accidents and sometimes deaths occurred because of the misuse of firearms and guns by gamekeepers and others during shooting parties. Guns could be as unpredictable as people and ammunition could cause a gun barrel to explode, so it was not always the user that was at fault.

Although the agricultural industry was considered the least regulated, there was some legislation which introduced safety measures. The first was the Threshing Machine Act in 1878 which meant that belts and machinery had to be protected. The Chaff Cutting Machines Act of 1897 imposed similar requirements. Despite increased mechanisation in the industry, agricultural workers had no statutory protection except the limited areas covered by both of the above mentioned Acts. It was unfortunate that the requirements enforced by the Factories Acts did not cover agriculture operations.

## Commercial fishing and whaling industry

Commercial fishing was one of the most dangerous jobs and posed a substantial risk of death or serious injury to those working in the industry. In the nineteenth century fishing smacks suffered heavy losses at sea. The small boats were gradually replaced by steam-powered trawlers and motor vessels which reduced the number of casualties and the loss of boats.

All but a few deaths of fishermen at sea were reported to the Registrar General of Shipping and Seamen – not the registrar general. Most individual accidents were as a result of drowning. Between 1861 and 1871 about 1,000 fishing smacks operated from ports on the east coast and approximately 120 such vessels and their crews were lost each year.

Many trawlers and drifters were lost at sea resulting in fatalities and injuries amongst their crews. Workers sometimes fell overboard; some men would be tangled up in nets and then be caught in the winches and some were just pulled underwater and drowned. Weather and rough seas often played their part when men and boys were swept overboard in vicious storms. Occasionally the boilers on steam-propelled boats would explode causing serious injuries and if boats collided, sometimes crew members became trapped and probably drowned. No wonder being a simple fisherman was considered such a dangerous job.

Whaling was even worse! It was an extremely dangerous industry but very profitable. The whaling ships normally operated alone and in far-flung corners of the globe and sometimes in uncharted oceans. Many small islands, particularly in the Pacific Ocean, were named by the whalers who discovered them.

The main dangers of whaling were as follows:

- being trapped in ice when sailing in the far north of Canada
- boats being crushed by trapped ice
- boats being smashed to pieces by whales
- fire from boilers rendering whale oil
- capsized boats
- drowning or lost at sea due to storms
- misuse of harpoons.

Whalers were not paid a wage as such; instead they usually received a share of the proceeds of the spoils or catch of the trip. Like many seagoing jobs, whaling was not an easy life; men could die of scurvy or suffer accidents from a variety of causes. They faced the prospect of death every day.

Whales did not typically sink whaling ships, but sometimes in their struggle to survive, they frequently caused the whaleboats to sink. Whaleboats were small boats with oars. Whalers would row out to the injured whale in these smaller boats once it had been harpooned. It was at that point that the struggling whale became extremely dangerous and could easily smash a whaleboat to pieces with one flick of its huge tail.

Whale oil was one of the main reasons for the whaling industry. The oil of course was flammable and could catch fire which meant that surface oil on the decks could spread to the barrels of oil stowed below. Leakage was also common so oil could seep into the bilges fuelling a big dangerous fire.

It could be said that commercial fishermen and whalers had an easier life than miners, industrial workers and the chimney sweeps' climbing boys because they worked outdoors in the fresh air – but it was many times more dangerous than those occupations. The sad fact is that, due to the very nature of their job and being so far from any coastline or land where help might be available, medical treatment was just not available so many died as a result.

## Dockyard and marine workers

Dock labourers fall into two distinct classes – *lumpers* and *stevedores*. The lumpers, helped by porters, unloaded cargo from ships and the stevedores loaded cargo onto ships for outgoing journeys.

Dock labouring was a precarious way of earning a living; in most port towns the supply of labour outweighed the demand. Many docks, which formed permanent berths for the larger shipping companies, employed men on a regular basis, but in other docks men were employed on a day or casual basis.

Sickness and accidents were common, and many accidents and injuries were sustained while handling heavy goods when loading or unloading ships at docks around the country – stevedores were amongst those most regularly injured. Many dock companies had no medical facilities although they were probably fairly close to a local doctor or hospital.

Shipwrights and those working on maintenance in the dry docks were also prone to accidents from failing cranes and winches or they could simply be knocked out because they collided with someone carrying a long plank of wood. Dockyards were notoriously poorly illuminated and poor weather conditions such as fog, mist, strong winds and lashing rain all reduced visibility which added to the dangers.

Dockyard workers were exposed to all weathers. The work was hard, labour-intensive and fraught with danger. Unloading cargoes such as grain or coal in confined conditions meant that workers were prone to various bronchial and pulmonary diseases. In addition, accidental deaths were common verdicts as a result of falling bales or broken slings; many fatal incidents happened too if a worker was accidentally stabbed with a hook, which was a tool of the trade.

The majority of docks were operated by privately owned commercial companies but railway companies also operated both docks and ferries together with other merchant shipping organisations, so it wasn't just dockyard workers that suffered accidents and injuries. Merchant seamen, railway employees and others working on the dockside could also be affected. In order to move the goods once offloaded from ships, the railway companies had open tracks in port areas so moving trains and shunting was a major hazard. The Royal Docks also employed large numbers of both naval personnel and civilian workers in maritime shipbuilding and other associated tasks.

There were many health issues associated with maritime work and the healthcare facilities provided for private shipyard and dock workers and Royal dockyard workers were mixed. Some workers were astute enough to join sick clubs, benefit societies and even burial societies. This gave them some sort of insurance; some also contributed to Hospital Saturday Fund schemes.

The Royal dockyards employed surgeons whose responsibilities increased significantly as medical and healthcare provisions developed. Naval authorities led the way in implementing advances in medical practice; surgeons treated the sick and injured but were also involved in other dockyard matters.

After 1881 naval surgeons from the Royal Hospital Haslar medical school visited naval dockyards in order to understand hygiene standards in relation to ship construction; but this was not the case of civilian surgeons in regard to commercial docks and shipbuilders. Admissions to the Albert

Dock Seamen's hospital for merchant sailors included those who suffered from accidents at the docks. London dock companies made allowances for employees injured at work.

Over time a better understanding of the difficulties experienced by all kinds of workers in dockyards, shipbuilding and the ports led to improved health care and better facilities.

## Drivers of horse-drawn carriages, wagons and carts

The trials and tribulations encountered on the roads during the nine-teenth century were many! One could be forgiven for thinking that that the growth of the railway system mitigated the need to use poor roads or tracks that criss-crossed the country, but there was a huge increase in the demand for wagons, carts and coaches or carriages right up to the early twentieth century. It was indeed the age of the horse – *not the iron horse*. Everything had to be transferred from rail to road at some point, be it people, goods or materials, so travelling by road could be a dangerous yet necessary activity.

Turnpike roads were roads where a toll was collected, supposedly for the upkeep of the road, but by the mid-1840s turnpike roads were not well-maintained at all and were on their way out because of the new railway system – but even that was decades away from connecting all areas to the rail system.

Many people were fearful about travelling at speed on this new form of transport on the roads. Travelling by road resulted in many injuries and deaths because many roads were actually just cart tracks. In addition, obviously where there were moving vehicles, there were accidents, and the most common causes were poor weather conditions, fast driving and drunkenness. The whole experience had *accident waiting to happen* written all over it!

Mailcoach drivers were renowned for swearing and drunkenness. They were employed by the independent companies who provided the coach to the Royal Mail in order to deliver letters. These coaches travelled at medium to high speeds and passengers chose this means of travel for that very benefit – definitely not for comfort. However, for passengers they were slightly more comfortable than stagecoaches which were often crowded and travelled at a slower speed. The mailcoach only stopped for delivery of mail and they were eventually phased out during the mid-1800s as they were replaced by trains as the railway network expanded.

During the era of the horse-drawn transport there were numerous reasons why accidents happened. The primary causes of carriage accidents were mainly related to aspects of driving, road conditions, horses, harnesses and the type and roadworthiness of the carriages:

- careless driving due to lack of attention
- driving while drunk
- driving up banks or into ditches by ignoring hazards
- lack of control of the horses
- poor road surfaces
- wheels getting trapped in ruts
- bolting horses
- harnesses breaking
- overloaded carriages could be pulled backwards going uphill
- speeding down a hill caused carriages to collide with the horses.

All these factors caused accidents, some of which were fatal. In 1833 the Liverpool Express Stagecoach overturned near Chalk Hill in Dunstable, Bedfordshire and a male passenger was killed. There are reports of such cases in newspapers and in official Quarter Sessions court records. Clearly there was a need for proper driving to prevent most carriage accidents. Not only were people injured but horses suffered injury or death too as a result.

Unfortunately there were no penalties as such for poor driving – many drivers were ignorant and inexperienced and had no idea how to control the horses. However, stiff penalties were imposed on employers of known drunken drivers. Intoxication was common and it was necessary to deter drunk drivers.

Accidents were also caused by obstacles on the road; in urban areas over-crowded streets and road works installing pipes were a hazard and in the countryside drivers had to be aware of fallen trees or overhanging branches to say nothing of loose stones and the inevitable potholes.

Although safety measures were never formally defined for carriage riding, passengers were advised to secure themselves so that they did not slide off their seat if there was any sudden movement or abrupt halt. They were also told to watch their step when getting in and out of carriages to prevent accidental falls – women in particular were advised to pay attention to their long skirts to prevent them from getting caught under foot or entangled within the steps. Passengers were also advised never to jump out of carriage while it was in motion, but if a horse bolted and the person wanted to get out too, they were advised to jump in the same direction that the horses were travelling.

A search of the British Newspaper Archive for carriage accidents in the last half of the nineteenth century revealed around 31,000 results. The results showed that most fatalities were due to head injuries and the causes of specific accidents are also given:

- broken harness resulting in the horse bolting, throwing occupants of the carriage out with one being accidentally kicked by the horse and killed
- horse bolted, carriage overturned, two of the five occupants killed
- horses bolted, carriage collided with empty wagon, overturned and was dragged along on its side with occupants injured
- horse stumbled, the carriage shafts hit pavement and threw occupants out of the carriage resulting in serious head injury
- horses bolted, occupants thrown, one was seriously injured with a broken arm and badly fractured and mangled leg as a consequence of being dragged
- coachman's seat and footboard detached and landed on horses which bolted, coachman was dragged and killed
- horses hit a tollgate which was not opened in time resulting in occupant thrown and killed, the horses were also badly injured.

By law each parish was responsible for the care and maintenance of its own roads. A Surveyor of Highways would be elected by the parish vestry and appointed each year. The surveyor could also claim the free use of horses, carts and tools, normally from the wealthier members of the community. It was also his responsibility to ensure that each parishioner provided a week's work every year to take care of parish roads.

## Railway workers and passengers

Most people believe that George Stephenson's *Rocket* was the first train ever built. This is not strictly true as earlier steam-powered engines made to run on rails had been invented and were used in the mining and other industrial settings. Stephenson's early locomotive was designed and built in 1829 and is the most famous example of early steam trains. The Rainhill Trials of the Liverpool and Manchester Railway (L&MR) held in October the same year demonstrated that these types of locomotive would be more efficient than stationary steam engines.

Of course, the general population were terrified out of their wits at this steaming noisy metal monster which had entered their lives; the entrepreneurs of the day were keen advocates of them while others were dead

*Devastation from a railway accident at Sutton Coldfield, Jan 1955*

against them at all costs. Arguments must have ensued but, as they say … the rest in history!!

In the early days of the railway industry there were many accidents and you only have to look in the records of the private railway companies to see the types of injuries sustained by both staff and passengers. Most accidents could have been avoided but they occurred because of a need to stick to timetables rigidly and to make sure rolling stock was in the right place. Safety was not considered important but both passengers and staff were victims of accidents. Accidents occurred for many reasons but could have been due to bad weather or because of infrastructure failures such as track and points failures. Both injuries and deaths occurred.

Any major accidents that occurred were published in the *Railways Gazette* and information can be viewed on the railways archive website and are summarised as well as showing reports of witnesses, plans and diagrams and other records. Many books have been written and are readily available on the topic of development of the railways in the nineteenth century.

Full details of legislation, accidents reports and records can be found in appendix 10.

## Canal workers
The Industrial Revolution required better transport of goods, and the golden age of canal building was from the 1770s through to the 1830s. Today, the canals are used largely for leisure but they were constructed in the age of pick and shovel. Those who did the manual work of digging channels, blasting rocks and construction were known as navigators, and this gave us the term *navvies*. Men lived on the job in temporary encampments where disease could rapidly spread. Not all local communities welcomed navvies and the stories of fights abound. Accidents were frequent and regarded as part of the job of building canals. Perusal of newspapers will find reports of more major incidents while local parish registers covering the time that a particular canal was constructed through a parish may provide details of burials, but some may be without any name.

From 1795, the Registry of Boats Act required all vessels on inland waterways to be registered. These records are to be found in Quarter Sessions. Some have been transcribed and published, such as those by the *Eureka Partnership*. Although many boats on canals were *Number Ones* operated by a family, others were operated by larger companies. If you know the company involved you may find records at The National Archives, local archives or in the Waterways Archives which may indicate when names changed to suggest a death.

Boat-operating families were often regarded with suspicion and referred to as *water gypsies*. Boatmen and their families, who plied their trade on the canals, were exposed to risks. Initially boats were largely manned by the crew, but once the railways presented competition for the transporting of freight, boatmen could not always afford a cottage so families moved onto the boats and all were involved with loading, unloading and getting the goods to their destination in a timely manner. While some canal accidents made the headlines, many did not. Regular incidents would involve drowning, crushing especially at locks, entanglement in ropes, etc. Again, if you know the canal routes plied by your ancestors, then it is the parish registers of the areas through which the canal threaded that you may details of cause of death. Local newspapers are a good source for incidents on the canals particularly if the coroner was involved. The Canal Boats Act of 1877 introduced an inspectorate due to concerns for the living conditions and morals of families living in confined space on the boats and some records may be found in local archives.

Headline-making accidents did occur. In 1818 a boat loaded with gunpowder exploded in Nottinghamshire causing deaths and extensive damage. Another resulted in a change to the law. A boat carrying a mixed cargo that included several tons of gunpowder along with other flammable materials exploded on the Regent's Canal in London killing all the crew, demolishing a bridge and causing extensive damage. The subsequent 1875 Explosives Act introduced restrictions on carriage of mixed cargoes that involved explosive materials.

If your ancestors worked the canals of the midlands of England, then it is always worth checking the parish registers for All Saints', Braunston. This Northamptonshire church was known as the *Cathedral of the Canals*.

Canal boats and those aboard were constantly on the move and this led on occasions to boatmen taking disease into a community, such as in 1834 when a boatman died of cholera at Braunston which led to some seventy persons being infected with nearly twenty deaths recorded in the village. In the early twentieth century, Sister Mary Ward became a legend for providing a free medical service for boat people from her home at Stoke Bruerne.

## Railway navvies

The railway navigators or *navvies* building Britain's railways had a reputation for hard drinking, petty thieving and womanising; they literally invaded towns and villages during the era of railway mania of the 1840s and beyond. Once their job was done, they then disappeared and moved on to the next contract. Without navvy labour the railways would not have been built and no matter where they lived, they occupied a prominent place in Victorian society.

A potted history of railway navvies can be seen at appendix 11 including details of records and reforms. What follows here are a few facts about navvies, their working conditions, the hazards they faced and the accidents and subsequent injuries they suffered:

- it took up to a year to train a labourer as a navvy
- navvying demanded strength and physical stamina
- navvies could shift twenty tons of earth in one day
- they worked with a pick, shovel and a wheelbarrow
- rock-blasting, spoil-tipping, ballasting and track-laying were also routine tasks
- navvies had a long working day with some men working during the night
- railway construction was very labour-intensive and a dangerous occupation

- speed as opposed to safety was the primary concern of the contractors
- navvies were prone to fatal accidents and severe injuries
- accidents were considered acceptable
- accidents occurred when building tunnels or using explosives for blasting
- companies or contractors never compensated the family of a navvy if he died
- contractors never made enquiries when men's limbs were blown off
- no provision was made by the company for accommodation of the sick.

In the early years of railway construction, it was thought that navvies were at greater risk of injury and death than a soldier on the battlefield.

Fatalities were commonplace often caused by working on inclines where people were either thrown from bogies or even just walking and being run over by railway trucks. Reports of coroners' inquests in provincial newspapers are very revealing and often damning of the circumstances of accidental deaths. Coroners and their jurors travelled to the railway to view the bodies of men killed in accidents, and in some locations a dead house (mortuary) was provided to house the corpses. When the men had an accident or were injured, they were often transported by horse and cart to hospital several miles away and some did not survive. Local graveyards can tell stories of deaths in railway navvy communities. Unmarked navvy graves exist in most areas, sometimes because actual names were never established.

Disease and epidemics were commonplace too within communities; smallpox was known to have been the case at Ribblehead on the Settle to Carlisle railway. There were also fights between the navvies resulting in injuries which sometimes left navvies unable to work; even murders took place, often in local hostelries.

In March 1882 one of my own ancestors, a railway navvy aged forty-seven, was involved in an accident on railway widening and tunnelling work at Wymington in Bedfordshire. He had been employed by Messrs Thomas and Young who were the contractors working for the Midland Railway Company for about three months. My ancestor was crossing the main running line, walking towards the village of Irchester, when he was knocked down by an express train and killed instantly. An inquest was held returning a verdict of accidental death.

At the inquest the body was identified by the Wymington shanty keeper and the train driver gave evidence saying it would have been impossible to avoid him as he was in charge of an express train travelling at about fifty miles an hour from London to Derby. Despite blowing the whistle it appears that this was ignored; however, it was perhaps not heard as my ancestor was deaf and also had a lung condition affecting his breathing.

## Other work-related accidents

Work-related injuries were commonplace and many workers in manufacturing and on the land suffered the effects of the noxious substances with which they had daily contact. All these circumstances took a massive toll on people's physical well-being and left men and women with poor health and ageing before their time.

Accidents and even fatalities were a daily occurrence in the hazardous Victorian workplace – people fetching water for the forge could fall into the river or well and be drowned or they could be accidentally killed when a cart went out of control.

Accidents at work were varied including falling from a ladder as a result of a broken rung, falls from scaffolding, falling from a haystack and being stabbed with the upturned prongs of a pitchfork or being suffocated by residual gasses when clearing a vat of the dregs of the stale ale in a brewing accident, steeplejacks falling from spires or being knocked out by bells, The extent and variety of accidents was vast but workers in certain trades such as building and transport were more at risk than others. Building trades seem to have topped the list for accidents which occurred in most of the occupations associated with the trade.

Transport seems to have accounted for a number of accidental deaths particularly carters and coachmen being injured or killed as a result of road accidents and they were often reported as being run over by their own wagons. Those looking after horses were also at risk from kicks while grooming which often proved fatal.

## Coroners' inquests

Coroners have been investigating work accidents for at least six centuries. In an inquest the coroner and the jury view the body of the deceased, examine witnesses and reach conclusions about the cause or manner of death, which may be as a result of an underlying cause and not the actual accident itself.

Coroners became salaried officials in 1860 and were paid per inquest *duly held*. In 1836 the Medical Witnesses' Act authorised coroners to pay a doctor up to two guineas to perform a post-mortem and give evidence. Immediately after civil registration in 1837, there was an increase in the numbers of inquests held because causes of death needed to be certified when involving a fatality as a result of a work-based accident. Many coroners, however, received a high proportion of their cases from hospitals and infirmaries which benefitted from free medical evidence because until 1926 doctors were not entitled to be paid to give evidence at an inquest where the subject was their patient.

A coroner's police officer had the power to rule out the need for medical evidence in cases of accident.

Inquests were held on all fatalities caused by accidents in the workplace. Some case files are held at The National Archives and many are held in county record offices, but not all survive. They are subject to a seventy-five-year closure but many coroners destroyed their records after fifteen years. In many cases more detailed information can often be found in local newspaper reports than official records.

Official records mainly comprise the indictment files held at The National Archives. For a short period (1487 to 1752) it was common for coroners to hand over records of inquests to assize judges.

The records of inquests normally contain three elements:

- inquisitions – the finding of the jury with a brief synopsis of the events leading up to death
- statements of evidence – sworn before the coroner and usually substantial
- other papers – lists of the jury members, the costs incurred by witnesses
- orders – made to hold persons who might have to face any criminal/negligence charges.

## Insurance industry involvement

An early type of insurance was available from the medieval monasteries. Those who could afford to do so purchased a *corrody* which would provide care either within the monastery itself or provide regular cash payments. (A *corrody* was essentially a lifetime allowance of food, clothing, shelter and care from an abbey, monastery or other religious institution.)

Before industrial insurance companies were established, ordinary people relied on the local craft and trade guilds or livery companies; they played a pivotal role in the provision of funds for their members and families in times of sickness or when they died. Friendly societies and burial clubs assured similar help for many and co-operatives and trades unions also participated.

Initially the commercial assurance companies catered for the wealthier members of society, but during the nineteenth and twentieth century, industrial assurance companies were replaced by life assurance companies. From the start of the twentieth century, many employers were also providing sick benefits to their workers.

Family historians need to ascertain if an ancestor had an insurance policy and which company or organisation held it. Researching the following will be beneficial in finding which company:

- wills
- death duty registers
- family papers
- company records.

When policies were taken out to provide for dependants in the event of sickness or death, you should find some or all of the following:

- names, ages and relationships
- occupations
- addresses
- information such as executors, guardians and bankruptcies.

More wealthy individuals may have had more than one policy – some on unrelated people who were ignorant of the fact that a policy covered them. Life policy interests were often auctioned during the last half of the Victorian era.

Researching the records of the local trade guilds, livery companies and various trades unions should also provide valuable information about ancestors. Many organisations which were involved in the relief of those who became ill or sick as a result of work related ailments have extensive archives.

During the late nineteenth century insurance against accidents at work started to become commonplace. The Railway Passengers Assurance Company, formed in 1848 in England, was believed to be the first company to offer this type of insurance cover with the object of insuring against the rising number of fatalities on the embryonic railway system. Known as the Universal Casualty Compensation Company, it granted assurances on the lives of persons travelling by railway and compensation where an accident was not fatal. Like all insurance though, there were conditions.

The insurance company agreed with the railway companies that their basic accident insurance would be sold with travel tickets as part of an optional package. Insurers would charge higher premiums for second- and third-class travel due to the higher risk of injury in the roofless and often inferior carriages.

The private insurance companies played a significant part in raising industrial safety standards both during and since Victorian times, not just on the railways but also in many other spheres of industry. Their engineers periodically carried out thorough examinations of steam-pressure vessels and all types of lifting machinery on the premises of the insured. Engineering surveyors then issued certificates of examination. It was then the responsibility of the district factory inspectors to enforce any required remedial actions.

Towards the end of the nineteenth century, steps were taken by the government in the form of the Workman's Compensation Act 1897. This introduced a scale of payments made by employers to employees who suffered injuries that arose from, and in the course of, employment. The Act only related to blue-collar industrial workers. It also set up an accident fund to which all men employed by a company were entitled to contribute. The scheme covered both fatal and non-fatal accidents and paid out weekly amounts. A further Act in 1906 expanded the scheme.

## Other legislation affecting working conditions

As technological advances were made and industries expanded, the government constantly had matters under review and several Acts of Parliament were passed and laws and new regulations introduced:

- the Workmen's Compensation Act of 1897 established that persons injured at work should receive a degree of compensation without having to prove that the employer was at fault
- by 1914, the hours and wages of textile workers improved
- young children no longer worked in the factories
- the Factory Acts were the main vehicles for improvement
- some factories increased the holiday provisions for their workers; local *wakes weeks* became common with whole factories heading to holiday destinations
- improvements as a result of legislation and improvements in the mines
- ventilation was improved by the installation of fans
- steam-powered pumps reduced the risk of flooding
- iron tracks introduced to make pushing the coal carts easier
- children now prevented from working down the mines
- pit ponies replaced children
- electric lighting introduced in some pits.

# CONCLUSION

Having rested and recharged our batteries after our fascinating journey through health care in volume one, we were all set for our second expedition. On reaching this point I think this second journey would be better described as *an escape and evasion exercise*!

We were hungry the first day due to famine in the land and held our noses through the *great stink*. Next we ploughed our way through the Black Death but thankfully managed to avoid the plague. Already we were becoming more cautious so we craftily bypassed some lepers, skirted round people infected with smallpox and cholera and mentally listed all the symptoms of diphtheria, phthisis and silicosis – and other diseases ending in *-itis*, *-isis* and *-oid*. We peeped inside some home medicine chests and were astonished at the contents, to say nothing of those Regency dandies we spotted with their ridiculous hairdos. Some of them would make excellent twenty-first-century drag queens!

Having survived the epidemics, we needed a day of rest so visited the nearest market town, but even that outing was hijacked by various silver-tongued, quick-talking quacks selling their pills, potions and universal mixtures which they claimed would cure any problem from earache to athlete's foot and everything in between – including more serious infections and internal diseases! We fled and ventured into what we thought would be a calmer more cultured atmosphere. Avoiding a couple of rebellions organised by Wat Tyler, we headed for the larger cities, drawn by the intriguing unusual sounds and smells which assailed our senses … what on earth was going on?

Industrialisation … that's what it was! Everywhere was a hive of activity and the noise was deafening; and the streets and sewers didn't exactly smell like a bed of roses either! Where men used to do the work manually, now everyone, including women and children, were tending their machines – machines which clamped and cut; drilled and drained; grooved and smoothed; powered and pumped and even moved iron monsters like locomotives! With clanking looms and flying shuttles, the place was a madhouse; ear-splitting noise competed with shouts and orders from overseers while children, toddlers even, grovelled around our feet underneath moving machines with a rag and oil can in their hand! The toxic smells were unbelievable. We beat a hasty retreat and headed for a quieter residential area.

Quaffing down a watery beer in the local alehouse, the chatty barmaid who only had one ear, a genetic deformity inherited from her grandpa, gave us all the local gossip. We were advised to absolutely avoid the opium dens and take the utmost care if we used a lavatory as they had a tendency to explode sometimes! We could not believe our ears; we were spellbound by her further tales of killer green wallpaper containing arsenic, exploding billiard balls and we should definitely not stay long in places lit by gas lamps because we could become unconscious. Even babies' bottles were known as murder bottles, she said. This was all too much – and I was down to my last tissue in the box! We came across a tattered copy of the *Book of Household Management* by Mrs Beeton – bedtime reading sorted! It turns out Mrs Beeton was a lady of common sense and explained how careful one had to be using cleaning products as they contained poisons and people should be aware of plastic brooches and hair combs – and even lead toy soldiers! And corpse candles apparently were deadly! Who knew?

On our way home, we passed coal, copper and tin mines but we politely declined the invitation from a ten-year-old to join him down the mine; neither did we fancy helping the stevedore and navvy near the railway or going on a whaling trip. We headed home, exhausted, hanging on for dear life as the tipsy stagecoach driver rattled along the turnpike as if he was trying to win horseracing's Gold Cup! So, yet again, it's been an expedition with a vengeance – yet we survived volume two. I am surprised Queen Victoria lived as long as she did through this hazardous era; at one point I began to wonder if anyone would be left in the world – but our forebears did survive for us to be here! Our third journey will take us … well, you'll just have to wait and see!

*If you have only read this volume, then now is the time to read volumes one, three and four to complete your journey through the lives of the ancestors and the health care available to them.*

# LIST OF ILLUSTRATIONS

1. A fashionable man takes his hat off while strolling and his hairdresser assists him by supporting the weight of his large wig – Coloured engraving by J. Caldwell after M. V. Brandoin. Wellcome collection. Public domain.

2. Scenes typical of life during the Black Death plague – Facsimile reproduction from a pictorial broadside of 1665-6. Wellcome Collection.

3. Medieval graffiti from time of the Black Death in the Church of St Mary the Virgin, Ashwell, Hertfordshire – Author's photograph.

4. Woman suffering smallpox. Pustular eruption of smallpox on face – Wellcome Collection. CC BY 4.0.

5. Cholera treatment equipment: portable apparatus for injecting saline solution – Photograph c.1910. Welcome Collection. Public domain mark.

6. Open air tuberculosis ward at the Royal Hospital Haslar – Photo 1914/1918, Wellcome Collection.

7. Bunhill Fields London, a typical overcrowded burial ground – © Jim Osley, Geograph/Creative Commons CC BY-SA 2.0.

8. Cross Bones burial ground Southwark – ProfDEH Wikimedia Commons CC BY-SA 4.0

9. Quacks at work. A patient sits helplessly in a chair while proponents of different medicines brawl with each other, overturning tables and chairs – Lithograph by C.J.Grant, 1834. Wellcome Collection. Public domain mark.

10. Phrenology – Dr. Guislain Psychiatry Museum, Gent. Creative Commons CC0 1.0.

11.  Opium dens typical of those frequented by sailors in East London – Illustration by W. D. Almond for Illustrated London News 6 Dec 1890.

12.  Death portrayed as a lethal confectioner making up sweets using arsenic and plaster of Paris as ingredients representing the toxic adulteration of sweets in the 1858 Bradford Sweets Poisoning – Wood engraving after J. Leech, 1858. Wellcome collection. Public domain mark.

13.  Child apprentices in textile factory. Apprentice greeting former friend, the workers in rags – Wellcome Collection. CC BY 4.0.

14.  Children working in mines – Image from: The physical and moral condition of the children and young persons employed in mines and manufactures / Illustrated by extracts from the Reports of the Commissioners. For inquiring into the employment of children and young persons in mines and collieries, and in the trades and manufactures. Wellcome Collection. Public domain mark.

15.  Arsenic furnace used in processing arsenic – Etching. Wellcome Collection. Public domain mark.

16.  Devastation from a railway accident at Sutton Coldfield, Jan 1955 – Midland Railway Study Centre

**Front cover additional images:** (top right) Parkers' Tonic, Wellcome Collection, public domain mark; (bottom left) Medicine bottles, Shutterstock.

# LIST OF APPENDICES

1. Medieval ailments and cures
2. Georgian and Regency ailments and cures
3. Holloway's Universal Ointment and Pills
4. Extract from a cholera prevention poster
5. A potted history of the first and second opium wars
6. Factory Acts and regulations to protect children and workers in textile mills
7. Legislation and reforms to protect chimney sweep climbing boys
8. Coal mining records, reforms and legislation
9. The Bevin Boys
10. Railway accidents, legislation, records and reforms
11. A potted history of railway navvies

# APPENDIX 1

## MEDIEVAL AILMENTS AND CURES

**Evil spirits in the head** – Surgeons cut a hole in the skull to release evil spirits trapped in the brain. They may also have cut out the part of the brain 'infected' with the evil spirits.

**Toothache** – Patients were advised to burn a candle close to the tooth thus causing the worms that are gnawing the tooth to fall out into a cup of water held by the mouth.

**Bloodletting** – Blood was drained from a certain place in the body to release bad blood. The use of leeches became common for this process in the late medieval period and continued into the Victorian period.

**Cauterisation** – A physician identified that part of the body which was affected so it could be cured by having a red-hot poker put on it.

**Astrology** – Astrology played an important part in many medieval cures. Anyone suffering from fever was bled immediately the moon passed through the middle of the sign of Gemini.

**Gout** – People were advised to make a mixture out of worms, pigs' marrow and herbs all boiled together and apply to the affected foot.

**Deafness** – If grease from a fox was mixed with the gall of a hare and warmed, and then placed in the ear, it would cure deafness.

**Smallpox** – Hanging red curtains around the bed was said to show red light and this would subsequently cure the patient.

**Head lice** – Pouring tobacco juice onto the scalp would kill head lice.

**Jaundice** – For one week patients should swallow a mixture of nine ales and soaked lice each morning.

**Baldness** – More grease from the fox used here. Bald people could smear grease from a fox into a bald scalp, shaving the head first if need be. Another remedy involved garlic; some recommended crushing garlic and rubbing it into the scalp after which the scalp was washed with vinegar.

**Plague** – Burn leather to produce smoke; the smoke supposedly killed off the plague.

# APPENDIX 2

## GEORGIAN AND REGENCY ERA AILMENTS AND CURES

**Baths** – The body was fully or partially plunged into liquid for various periods. There were three reasons given for having baths: dermal or cutaneous (skin) absorption, for "exciting" the skin and as an emollient or aromatic aid. Baths were also used for cerebral afflictions where the patient sat in a bath of warm water while being drenched in cold water. Water showers were commonly used in asylums for the early treatment of the insane.

**Blistering or vesiculation** – This process raised a blister on the skin and was supposedly used to correct a wide variety of health problems including hysteria, gout, inflammation and fevers.

**Boluses or pills** – The difference between boluses and pills related to their weight. Boluses weighed more than six grains and pills weighed less than six grains. (A grain was a weight used in troy, avoirdupois and apothecaries' systems.) They were used in treatments as astringents, diuretics and purgatives as well as being prescribed for conditions including epilepsy, fevers, delirium and dropsy.

**Collyria** – Liquid eye washes (collyria) were created from infusions or distilled waters. Infusion involved extracting chemical compounds from plants in water, oil, or alcohol and then applied externally using an eye bath to give relief.

**Enemata (Enema)** – This was used as a purgative in the intestinal tract and injected in small quantities for abdominal inflammation in order to reduce swelling. They were also used to treat diarrhoea, constipation and dysentery.

**Fomentations** – These were sponged applications to the body of tepid fluid prepared from infusions from narcotic plants containing substances that caused unusual inflammation and then depression of the central nervous system. Most of the plants used were highly toxic.

**Fumigations** – These vapours basically purified the air. Medical vapours were used to treat various skin diseases and to help with the treatment of venereal disease where the skin was affected. There were different kinds of fumigations depending on the ailment.

**Gargle** – These were preparations used to treat throat or mouth ailments. Different

124

kinds of gargles such as antiseptics or even detergents were used. Users let the gargle to rest on the affected parts by tilting their head back and not swallowing the gargle.

**Injections** – These liquid compositions were injected into external auditory passages, the urethra, the bladder, and other fistular cavities. They were used to treat chronic discharges that caused debility.

**Liniments** – These were oil-based liquid preparations rubbed into any affected area of the body, sometimes used as stimulants and for chronic rheumatic pains. They were also used for rickets and nervous pains. People today still use gels and creams to ease rheumatic pains.

**Ointments** – Ointments were perfectly smooth and applied externally to wounds or ulcers.

**Potions and powders** – These were liquid preparations often referred to as tonics; they were composed of infusions to which syrups, extracts, powders, or salts were added. They had multiple functions including use as laxatives, cough expectorants, and to give relief in cases of convulsions, epilepsy, digestive issues, fevers, dropsy, inflammation and severe pain. Powders were suspended in liquid or added to pastes for both internal and external use to treat cases of fever, venereal diseases and diarrhoea.

**Poultice or cataplasm** – These were made from pulps and powders combined with either water, milk or the liquor in which an animal or a vegetable substance has been boiled. They were warm and placed over affected areas of the body.

# APPENDIX 3

## HOLLOWAY'S UNIVERSAL MEDICINES

Thomas Holloway was a Victorian entrepreneur who made a fortune from the sale of his patent medicines, pills and ointments, designed to cure all ills. He was born in 1800 and by 1816 his parents had moved from Devonport to Penzance where his father kept the *Turk's Head* public house. Holloway entered into an apprenticeship with a local chemist between 1816 and 1820.

In 1828 he embarked on a career as a merchant and in 1836 set up both a business and home in London. In early 1829 he met an Italian leech vendor named Felix Albinolo who, at the time, was marketing his *St Cosmas and St Damian* ointment which claimed to cure a variety of different ailments and diseases. It was supposedly backed by testimonials from members of the medical profession.

In 1837 Holloway began advertising his own *Holloway's Universal Family Ointment* in *The Sunday Times,* following which Holloway and Albinolo competed in the newspaper advertising columns. Shortly afterwards, Holloway was imprisoned in Whitecross Debtors' Prison only to be bailed out by his mother in 1839. Not long after his release from debtors' prison, he began making pills to add to the Holloway brand. In January 1840 Holloway married Jane Pearce, the eldest daughter of a Rotherhithe shipwright. Jane died in 1875 but was heavily involved in the business.

Holloway's pills and ointment in subsequent years were a bounding success mainly due to his ability to publicise his patent medicines worldwide. He spent vast amounts of money on advertising including stamps and posters. He also enlisted agents throughout the British Empire and in other countries.

His pills and ointment were advertised as being a *universal cure* for almost any illness or disease and were used by thousands of people throughout the Victorian period, including Queen Victoria herself. His medicines were supposed to be able to cure asthma, bilious complaints, blotches on the skin, colic, constipation, consumption, debility, dysentery, female irregularities, fevers, fits, gout, headache, indigestion, inflammation, jaundice, liver complaints, lumbago, piles, rheumatism, urine retention, sore throats, tumours, ulcers, sexually transmitted disease, and worms! That's quite some claim!

Over the next sixty years the Holloway's business expanded due to the popularity of his ointment and pills with the Victorian public. However, medical professionals claimed that Holloway was a quack and a charlatan; an article published by the *Chemist and Druggist* in 1880 stated that the effectiveness of the medicines was highly questionable. The ingredients used were a closely-guarded secret until 1880 when the article also stated that ingredients of the pills and ointment were made from aloes, rhubarb root and ginger, various spices including cinnamon, cardamom, saffron, Glauber's salt and potassium sulphate, combined with a confection of roses. The ingredients used were not unusual at the time as society had not started to delve into the researching and testing new medicines. Nearly all the pills and ointments that were available in Victorian pharmacies consisted of herbs and plants, most of which had been used for medicinal purposes since medieval times. The great success of Holloway's pills and ointment was largely due to the vast amount of time and money that Holloway put into advertising his medicines.

From 1860 Holloway took a backseat from his business and moved to Tittenhurst Park in Sunninghill although he still spent many hours each day monitoring his business activities because it was still a very important part of his life. He had become a self-made millionaire and one of the richest men in the country, but with no children to inherit his fortune, he invested in philanthropic ventures.

For his first venture he built a sanatorium for 240 middle-class mentally ill patients in Virginia Water, Surrey, which was opened by the Prince and Princess of Wales in 1885. His wife, Jane, died in 1875, the cause of death being heart trouble and bronchitis. In her memory he embarked on his second philanthropic venture and built a college in Egham in Surrey to educate 250 middle-class women. Holloway died from congestion of the lungs before its opening by Queen Victoria in 1886.

# APPENDIX 4

## CHOLERA PREVENTION AND ADVICE POSTER

Cholera was widespread at times so the government created large posters which were widely distributed across the country. It included information about taking precautions and some recommended remedies. The following is extracted from one of the widely circulated posters.

1. *We would urge the necessity, in all cases of Cholera, of an instant recourse to medical aid, also under every form and variety of indisposition; for, during the prevalence of this epidemic, all disorders are found to merge in the dominant disease.*

2. *Let immediate relief be sought under disorder of the bowels especially, however slight. The invasion of Cholera may thus be readily and at once prevented.*

3. *Let every impurity, animal and vegetable, be quickly removed to a distance from the habitations such as slaughterhouses, pig-sties, cesspools, necessaries, and other domestic nuisances.*

4. *Let all uncovered drains be carefully and frequently cleansed.*

5. *Let the grounds in and around the habitations be drained, so as effectually to carry off moisture of every kind.*

6. *Let all partitions be removed from within and without habitations, which unnecessarily impede ventilation.*

7. *Let every room be daily thrown open for the admission of fresh air, and this should be done about noon, when the atmosphere is most likely to be dry.*

8. *Let dry scrubbing be used in domestic cleansing, in place of water.*

9. *Let excessive fatigue and exposure to damp and cold, especially during the night, be avoided.*

10. *Let the use of cold drinks, and acid liquors, especially under fatigue, be avoided or when the body is heated.*

11. Let the use of cold acid fruits and vegetables be avoided.

12. Let excess in the use of ardent and fermented liquors and tobacco be avoided.

13. Let a poor diet, and the use of impure water in cooking, or for drink, be avoided.

14. Let the wearing of wet and insufficient clothing be avoided.

15. Let a flannel or woollen belt be worn around the belly. This has been found serviceable in checking the tendency to bowel complaint so common during the prevalence of Cholera. The disease has, in this country, been always found to commence with looseness in the bowels, and in this stage is very tractable. It should, however, be noticed that the looseness is frequently unattended by pain or uneasiness, and fatal delay has often occurred from the notion that cholera must be attended with cramps. In the earlier stage here referred to, there is often no griping or cramp, and it is at this period that the disease can be most easily arrested. In all such cases let from twenty to forty drops of Dr. J Lenacs Cholera Tincture be administered in half a glass of brandy, and the symptoms will abate immediately.

16. Let personal cleanliness be carefully observed.

17. Let every cause tending to depress the moral and physical energies be carefully avoided.

18. Let crowding of persons within houses and apartments be avoided.

19. Let sleeping in low damp rooms be avoided.

20. Let fires be kept up during the night in sleeping or adjoining apartments, the night being the period of most danger from attack, especially under exposure to cold or damp.

21. Let all bedding and clothing be daily exposed during winter and spring to the fire, and in summer to the heat of the sun.

22. Let the dead be buried in places remote from the habitation of the living.

*Everyone should provide themselves with the Asiatic Cholera Tincture, as the most ready and effectual Remedy in Cholera, Diarrhoea, Flatulency, Cholic, and Bowel Complaints.*

*In bottles at 2s.9d, 4s 6d, 11s, and 21s. Duty included.*

*Also*

*The Anti-Cholera Fumigators, for purifying Air of Dwellings, and destroying the Contagious influence of cholera, typhus fever, and other infectious diseases. They are particularly recommended for the Sick Chambers, Hospitals, Churches, Chapels, Literary Institutions, Theatres, Assembly Rooms, Counting Houses, Taverns, the Cabins and Holds of Vessels, etc. In Boxes, at 6d, one shilling and 2s.6d each.*

*Anti-cholera tincture depot, 44, Coleman Street, London.*

# APPENDIX 5

## A POTTED HISTORY OF THE FIRST AND
## SECOND OPIUM WARS BETWEEN BRITAIN AND CHINA

The First Opium War was fought between the British and the Chinese from 1839 to 1842. There had been substantial growth in the export of opium in the year 1820 after the colonisation of India. This in turn resulted in increased opium addiction which totally disrupted the social lives of the people. It destroyed many families and households so the government of China started to confiscate opium in the year 1839 because of the havoc it caused.

More than 20,000 chests of opium were destroyed, most of which were found in the warehouses of the British merchants in Canton. This caused chaos. The war was sparked off when some drunken British merchants killed a Chinese man; they then refused to present themselves in the Chinese courts or accept any kind of punishment. Some British warships destroyed the Chinese barricades around the Pearl River estuary in Hong Kong and destroyed it, and in May 1841 the British captured the city after months of reinforcing their manpower, finally attacking the Chinese officials. A year later, Chinese troops attacked the British because they captured Nanking but the fighting came to an end.

The Second Opium War was fought by the British and French against the Chinese between 1856 and 1860. The Qing Dynasty was involved in ending the rebellion of Taiping which lasted about fourteen years until 1864. The British wanted to extend the right to do more trade in China, but this caused trouble. In 1856 Chinese officials boarded the *Arrow,* a British registered ship and arrested Chinese crew members which began a rebellion so the British again bombarded the Pearl Estuary after which all existing trade activities ceased. The British used the fact that a French missionary had been murdered by the Chinese to include the French in the war. Canton was captured primarily because the Chinese had fewer resources compared to the combined forces of the British and French. In 1858 British troops entered Tianjin and forced trade negotiations with the Chinese. Under the Treaty of Nanking in 1842, Hong Kong became a British colony. In 1857 the war resulted in the Treaties of Tianjin allowing Britain and France to recruit cheap Chinese labour. These Chinese emigrated and settled in their own enclave in the East End of London; they worked in the docks and with port shipping. As time progressed those industries declined and many set up restaurants or laundries.

In the 1860s various individuals and religious organisations began to campaign against unrestricted opium trafficking and there emerged heavy prejudice against the East End Chinese community initiated by the then popular press and even as a result of the writings of Charles Dickens in his portrayal of nineteenth-century London. At Pennyfields, there was a Christian mission and a Confucian temple. At Limehouse Causeway there was the famous Ah Tack's lodging-house.

# APPENDIX 6

## FACTORY ACTS AND REGULATIONS TO PROTECT CHILDREN AND WORKERS IN TEXTILE MILLS

Adults and children working in textile mills were often employed for long hours in appalling conditions for poor pay. In the majority of mills, they were exploited by ruthless owners who had no real regard for their workers – all they were interested in was profit! Legislation was eventually brought forward to improve the situation. Some Acts were specific to textile mills while others were more generic and affected all industrial units.

### Health and Morals of Apprentices Act 1802
The purpose of this Act was to give some protection for apprentices who were often orphans and lived and worked within the factory environment. Apprentices had to be housed in good accommodation and were restricted to working twelve hours a day. It also laid down how they could access education and religious observance. However, the Act was generally ignored as it could not be enforced. It was only relevant to apprentices so did not cover children who often worked alongside their parents and in most cases outnumbered the apprentice workers. The Act only applied to cotton mills.

### Factory Act 1819
No child under the age of nine was to work in the mills. Children between the ages of nine and thirteen years could only work a maximum of forty-eight hours each week and were required to go to school part-time. Again it only applied to cotton mills. There was no official method of enforcement because factory inspectors were not created at the time to investigate and enforce.

### Factory Act 1833
This Act further enforced the conditions of the 1819 Act. Factory inspectors were created to enforce the law but there were only four individuals to cover the whole of the country! Both parents and doctors lied about the ages of children and schooling was frequently avoided. If factory bosses were prosecuted for contravening the Act, any fines imposed were usually low.

## Factory Act 1878

This Act consolidated all the former Acts and applied to all trades. No child under the age of ten years could be employed. Education for children up to ten years old became compulsory and those between ten and fourteen years could only be employed for half days. Women were unable to work more than fifty-six hours per week. There was an increase in the number of inspectors but they had to cover the more than 110,000 workplaces, monitor around 3,000 textile mills and had the power to enter the mills and question workers.

Factory inspectors were able to devise new local regulations and laws to ensure the conditions required by the Factories Act were met and enforced; they also influenced legislation concerning machinery safety and reporting accidents. Changes to legislation between 1860 and 1871 saw the Factories Acts applied to virtually all manufacturing workplaces and the inspectors also became "technical advisers" as well as having an enforcement role.

Records of the Factory Inspectorate are held at The National Archives in series LAB and cover the period 1836-1975. They include:

- factory registers and certificates of employment
- files relating to the employment of women and young persons
- investigative reports on the many accidents which occurred almost daily.

# APPENDIX 7

## LEGISLATION AND REFORMS TO PROTECT CHIMNEY SWEEPS' CLIMBING BOYS

Climbing boys were very young children employed by chimney sweeps to climb up the inside of chimneys brushing and scraping them to clean them as they climbed to the top. They were often orphans so they were exploited ruthlessly at times.

Some poor parents even sold their children to a chimney sweep and many parents lied about their children's ages because smaller children were more desirable. Many climbing boys were not paid because the sweep supposedly provided basic board and lodging.

In 1788 legislation decreed that no child under the age of eight years would be allowed to be a chimney climbing boy although this was almost completely ignored.

In 1806 the Climbing Boys' Society promoted the use of brushes and rods as a viable alternative to children and lobbied parliament accordingly.

After the formation of the Climbing Boys' Society and by 1817, the movement began to do away with climbing boys although they were still needed. Old houses existed and many people felt that using climbing boys was the only proper way of cleaning their chimneys. Reforms were needed because chimney sweeps preferred smaller children because they could climb smaller chimneys. Girls as well as boys were used.

In 1834 a new Act was introduced stating that a child must express his own desire in front of a magistrate to be a chimney boy and that he was willing to work for his employer. The Chimney Sweeps Act 1834 made it illegal for anyone under the age of fourteen to climb up a chimney or for a boy under ten to be an apprentice chimney sweep. Information may be found in local Quarter Session records.

In 1840 an Act of parliament was passed which stated that no one under the age of twenty-one was permitted to climb chimneys. In the past, many children were forced to do so! This now stopped.

From 1875 local police forces issued annual licences to chimney sweeps making it illegal to trade without a licence. This important Act was prompted by the death of a young climbing boy in London's Shaftesbury hospital, and thus brought about the end of the chimney climbing boys.

There are records about accidents which happened to climbing boys in Board of Trade papers at The National Archives.

# APPENDIX 8

## COAL MINING RECORDS, REFORMS AND LEGISLATION

Safety legislation did not really begin to make the mines safer until the passing of the Coal Mines Act in 1842. The main provision of this Act was to prohibit women and children from working underground. It also set up the role of Inspector of Mines and Collieries. Further legislation followed with the Coal Mines Inspections Act 1850 which gave the mine inspectors rights to enter and inspect mine premises. However, it was not until the Mines Act of 1911 that full statutory powers were given to the inspectors.

Government departments with responsibility for the coal mining industry changed over time. Originally the mines inspectorate was the responsibility of the Home Office but in 1920 the Board of Trade took over that responsibility and set up a specific department to do so. Some mines and quarries were on land owned by the Crown, the Duchy of Cornwall or the Duchy of Lancaster. During the First World War the government increased its control over mines and mineral resources.

The inspectors' responsibilities were extended by a succession of statutes:

- Mines Act 1860 – ironstone mines
- Metalliferous Mines Regulation Act 1872
- Stratified Ironstone Mines (Gunpowder) Act 1881
- Slate Mines (Gunpowder) Act 1882
- Quarries Act 1894.

The Quarries Act 1894 gave inspectors the overall responsibility for all quarries. Previously factory inspectors had been responsible for some quarries but only those where they used steam power.

During the Industrial Revolution coal mining was one of the country's main industries and by 1911 there were around 3,000 mines employing over one million miners.

The Coal Mining History Resource Centre is an important resource giving a glimpse into the lives of coal-mining ancestors and their social and working conditions. The site also has a searchable database of over 200,000 recorded coal-mining accidents and deaths. Ancestry has the index of coal-mining accidents and deaths between 1878 and 1935 compiled by the Coal Mining History Resource Centre.

The index provides limited details of individuals affected including:

- name
- event type (accident or death)
- residence date
- residence place
- colliery
- owner
- brief details of event/notes.

The Coal Mining History Resource Centre database lists all recorded disasters since 1707. Pre-1850 there was no systematic recording of mining deaths. The records are very scattered. The information is somewhat sparse and is sourced from lists of victims from mining disasters, periodicals and newspapers of the time. Between 1850 and 1914 the lists of deaths are mainly taken from the Mines Inspectors' Reports. The reports covered deaths and some injuries in coal and metal mines as well as quarries. Official recording of names means there are about 90,000 people in the reports.

The number of accidents reported in each time span is as follows:

- 1700–1750    93
- 1750–1800    267
- 1800–1850    3,486
- 1850–1900    59,580
- 1900–1950    84,331.

Lancashire suffered the most disasters and casualties closely followed by Glamorgan, Durham and Yorkshire. Obviously other mining areas also suffered their share of casualties.

To access the database you will need to know the surname of the miner, location of the pit and if possible the approximate year. The website also includes transcripts of the 1842 Royal Commission reports which are also very revealing for background and historical information.

If employee records for the mine companies have survived they will more than likely be held by local record offices and may provide listings of the employees.

Online collections of the National Coal Mining Museum include photographs and descriptions of coal mining related items, letters, accidents and machinery. The library catalogue is also searchable online.

Mining has always been a dangerous occupation: between 1873 and 1953, there were around 85,000 deaths in the industry. The main source of information about accidents is the annual report of HM Inspector of Mines which commence in 1851. Accidents in ironstone mines were included from 1872, metalliferous mines from 1873 and quarries from 1894.

Reports exist for different regions of the UK including an overview and statistical information about accidents and their causes. For each accident up to 1914 there are lists of everyone who died and often there is an extensive description sometimes drawing on coroners' inquests reports. After the 1880s there were specific inquiries into major incidents and separate reports were made.

Records relating to the Inspector of Mines organised by districts are held at The National Archives in series POWE covering the period 1850-1968. The entry books in series HO95 cover 1855-1871 and the Factory and Mines' entry books cover the period 1843-1855. The North of England Institute of Mining and Mechanical Engineers, Nicholas Wood Memorial Library, also has copies of the Mines Inspectors' reports. The reports list fatalities by name and often include information on those injured but not killed.

Findmypast has an online database of Mining Disaster Victims taken from the Database of Fatalities in the Coal Fields covering Derbyshire, Leicestershire, Nottinghamshire, and Yorkshire. Each transcript provides some or all of the following:

- first and last name(s)
- birth year and age
- event date
- name of colliery
- incident details.

The National Union of Mineworkers' records are held by the union at their head office in Barnsley and these may provide more information about individual miners. You need to contact them directly for more information. The union also has records for the following former unions:

- 1889 the Miners' Federation of Great Britain was formed
- In 1932 it changed to the Mineworkers' Federation of Great Britain
- In 1945 it became the National Union of Mineworkers
- The South Wales Miners' Federation was formed in 1898 becoming the National Union of Mineworkers, South Wales area
- The Yorkshire Miners' Association was formed in 1881
- In 1889 became a founder member of the Miners' Federation of Great Britain
- In 1864 the Northumberland Miners' Mutual Confident Association was formed and became the Northumberland area of National Union of Mineworkers
- In 1844 the Lancashire Miners' Federation was formed and in 1897 it changed to the Lancashire and Cheshire Miners' Federation.

Some records of branches of the former unions may also be held at county record offices.

# APPENDIX 9

## THE BEVIN BOYS

At the start of the Second World War, the Government had underestimated the value of the younger coal miners without regard to their importance in the mining industry, so many were conscripted into the armed forces. This led to a shortfall of 36,000 workers. The government asked for volunteer conscripts to work in the mines but few responded; this shortage of manpower in the mines was a crisis. Some 720,000 men were needed in the mines to ensure an adequate supply of coal to the military and navy.

By October 1943 the government desperately wanted to safeguard coal supplies; shortages would affect the industrialised war effort and people in their own homes needing warmth in the winter. The government then announced that a proportion of conscripts would be redirected to the mines and this is how and why the Bevin Boys were established. The name *Bevin Boys* derives from the then Minister of Power, Ernest Bevin.

These young men conscripted to work in the coal mines were subject to a ballot draw when only ten per cent of conscripts between eighteen and twenty-five were chosen, together with volunteers who exercised an option as an alternative to military conscription. There were around 48,000 Bevin Boys who fulfilled a largely unrecognised service in the mines, most of whom continued to serve for a further two years after the end of the war. The initial aim was to assign the conscripts to training centres and mines as close to their homes as possible although logistically this became almost impossible to achieve.

Mines were dangerous places to work even in the twentieth century and many Bevin Boys suffered from accidents and injury. The first Bevin Boy killed in a mining accident was Henry Robert Hale who had only been at work for one month after his training when he was killed. Bevin Boys who were disabled by mining accidents did not receive any form of pension and nor were any provisions made for the dependents of any killed.

Many Bevin Boys suffered taunts because they did not wear a uniform; people wrongly assumed that they were deliberately avoiding military conscription. Conscientious objectors were also sent to work down the mines as an alternative to military service so there was sometimes an assumption that Bevin Boys were all *conchies* too.

The Bevin boy training centres included those located at:

- Creswell Colliery, Derbyshire.
- Haunchwood Colliery, Nuneaton, Warwickshire
- Newton Colliery, Clifton, Lancashire
- Askern Main Colliery, Doncaster, Yorkshire
- Prince of Wales's Colliery, Pontefract, Yorkshire
- Morrison Colliery, Southmoor, Durham
- Ollerton, Nottinghamshire.
- Horden Colliery, Durham
- Canterbury, Kent
- Cramlington Lamb Colliery, Northumberland.
- Birley Colliery (East Pit), Woodhouse, Yorkshire
- Oakdale Colliery, South Wales.

Bevin Boys were supplied with helmets and steel-capped safety boots and wore the oldest clothes they could find. Being of military age and without uniform, many were stopped and questioned by the police about avoiding call-up. The Bevin Boy programme ended in 1948 but they did not receive medals nor did they have the right to return to their pre-war jobs unlike armed forces personnel.

There were complaints from the outset about the wages paid. Their weekly pay was forty-four shillings per week which was insufficient to cover living costs. A number of Bevin Boys in Doncaster went on strike for two days before their training had finished in protest of the amount paid. Experienced miners also complained that the rate paid to an inexperienced twenty-one-year-old Bevin Boy was the same minimum wage that they received.

Unfortunately, call-up records for Bevin Boys were destroyed during the 1950s except those of the Midland Region which include about 8,000 names. Amongst the Ministry of Labour and National Service archive are several records relating to the Bevin Boys, the most pertinent being the register of coal mining ballots in series LAB 45/93 held by The National Archives. This record includes:

- names
- a number (presumably the person's number on the call-up list?)
- dates of selection
- location sent to.

# APPENDIX 10

## RAILWAY ACCIDENTS, LEGISLATION, RECORDS AND REFORMS

Ever since commercial railways began in the 1830s there was a heightened concern about accidents involving passengers due to different standards in the various railway operating companies. As a result, early legislation in the form of the 1840 Railway Regulation Act established the Railway Department of the Board of Trade and the appointment of Railway Inspectors. The Act also imposed responsibilities on railway companies to provide statistical information about passenger accidents. Until the last decade of the nineteenth century, the majority of investigations only related to passenger accidents but after 1890, inspectors were appointed specifically to investigate accidents involving employees.

All accidents were recorded and investigated by the Railway Inspectorate.

The accident reports whether dealing with fatalities or injury would record:

- date and time
- place
- name of individual injured or killed
- circumstances of the accident occurring
- verdict of inquest or inquiry
- recommendations to prevent same recurring
- remarks.

The major accidents that occurred were published in the *Railways Gazette* and information can be viewed on the railways archive website and are summarised as well as showing reports of witnesses, plans and diagrams and other records.

Many railway companies kept separate registers or record summaries of all accidents as they wanted to keep a record of how much time their employees were off work and the nature of their injuries. The records kept by each company varied but the majority are comprehensive despite being kept for the company's own purposes.

Records of accidents, inquests etc. were also kept by the railway trades unions as inevitably they made some benefit payment to next of kin to help with funeral expenses. The records would include:

- particulars of member (branch of the union, name, occupation)
- accident (date, type of accident, outcome – killed or injured)
- inquest (date, attended by – union representative, verdict).

Similar company records were kept where passengers were injured or killed on the railway. One of my own ancestors was killed because of a railway accident and by way of illustration brief details of the accident are recorded below:

In early September 1898 at Wellingborough railway station in Northamptonshire, a local postman took a mailcart to the station with mail to be loaded onto a train due at around 8.30pm. The mail should then have been taken to the down platform through a passageway which was gated, kept locked and located between the station yard and the platform. The postman went into the station, collected a luggage trolley and took it along the platform to the gate. At this point the platform sloped towards the tracks. The postman let go of the trolley and unlocked the gate – and whilst doing so the trolley ran off the platform onto the mainline track.

The postman and station foreman tried to move the trolley from the track but a London to Manchester express was due. A stationary train in the up platform blocked them moving the trolley onto the up-line and the trolley couldn't be moved back onto the platform. Both men had to jump for their lives as the express train approached.

The leading bogie of the locomotive derailed because it hit the trolley but the driving wheels did not derail so the engine continued until it hit a diamond crossover to the north of the station when it completely derailed ending up facing backwards. The first passenger coach was wrecked which resulted in the footplate crew and five passengers in that carriage being killed.

The Board of Trade accident investigation stated that *the down platform sloped unnecessarily steeply towards the track and the passageway gradient, although not as steep, still sloped to the track. Tests showed that the gradients were sufficient to allow a luggage trolley to roll away controlled. The inspector recommended that station platforms should either be level or slope away from the railway lines and that luggage trolleys used on station platforms should have brakes.*

In order to understand the role of the Rail Inspectorate it is necessary to understand their history. The body originated in 1840 when Inspecting Officers of Railways were first appointed by the Board of Trade.

Under the Railway Regulation Act of 1840, the Board of Trade had powers to appoint an inspector general and two inspectors of railways who reported on the construction, infrastructure, rolling stock and locomotives of new railways; they were also authorised to delay the opening of any railway until requirements were met. The Regulation of Railways Act of 1871 gave inspectors the statutory authority to investigate accidents and hold public inquiries. Accident inquiries where railway staff were involved had been investigated since 1858, but the Railway Employment (Prevention of Accidents) Act of 1900 authorised the Board of Trade to appoint inspecting officers to investigate the more serious accidents to employees.

The National Archive reference RAIL 1053 includes UK railway accident reports from 1853 to 1975 covering accidents from major train crashes to workers' minor injuries. These reports originated with the Board of Trade and were presented to Parliament. Many include witness statements from passengers and other railway workers.

Railway Inspectorate reports are also held at The National Archives in series MT29 covering the period from 1840 to 1964 and indexed in series MT29 and 30. Most of the original reports and files are in series MT6. Supplementary to these are the series files in MT114 but these are really only twentieth-century documents.

Throughout Britain the railways were then run by private companies but the 1840 Act required them to report all accidents which involved injury or death to the Board of Trade. The Act also gave the inspectorate powers to inspect any railway and to investigate serious railway accidents. Part of their work was inspecting new lines to determine whether they were suitable for carrying passengers or not.

Their first investigation was the Howden rail crash on 7 August 1840 which killed five people; the derailment of a train caused by the fall of a large casting from a wagon on a passenger train.

Inspectors were all recruited from the Royal Engineers. After the Railway Regulation Act 1871, the Board of Trade set up a formal court of inquiry to investigate accidents, taking evidence on oath from witnesses and making the hearings public. Inspectors investigating an accident were also required to make a formal report to the Board of Trade and publish the results.

During the mid-nineteenth century the Railway Inspectorate had three safety measures established to ensure passenger safety, summed up as *Lock, Block and Brake.*

- Lock – interlocking of points and signals, so that conflicting signals were prevented
- Block – a space-interval where a train was not allowed to enter a section of track until the preceding one had left it
- Brake – continuous brakes, to put at the command of the engine driver adequate braking power.

Most companies relied on their rule book as a solution to safety problems. At the start of World War One companies issued illustrated safety booklets to all their staff. However, as a result of trade union intervention, the regulations introduced under the 1900 Railway Employment (Prevention of Accidents) Act were far-reaching in some of the changes imposed which included:

- steam brakes on engines
- protection of gauge glasses in loco cabs
- illumination of shunting areas
- brake levers and labels on wagons,
- use of tow ropes to move wagons,
- provision of protective covers to exposed point rods and signal wires
- safety protection for permanent way workmen.

The Railway Work, Life and Death project is working to increase access to information about both British and Irish railway workers' accidents from about the 1880s up to 1940. The volunteers on this project collect and collate details of the accidents and making them available to everyone. (See website listing.)

The project makes use of the accident reports of the Railway Inspectorate because these give details of investigations into both major and minor railway worker accidents. The accident reports are an under-used but rich source of the numerous accidents; they also often reveal detail about working conditions, relationships between the government, the railway companies and the various trades unions and other people involved in accidents and who helped to change philosophies about safety standards.

As part of the project, information has been extracted from records including Railway Company Benevolent Fund books and the accident record books of the railway companies together with trade union records. The data is currently available as downloadable spreadsheets.

# APPENDIX 11

## A POTTED HISTORY OF RAILWAY NAVVIES

The term *navvy* originated in the mid-1700s and had a very precise meaning derived from the building of England's commercial canals which were known as navigations. When the canals were being built, there were no established civil engineers and consequently those labourers tasked with building them became known as *navigators* or *navvies* because they exercised a role in plotting a course for these waterways. When canal construction declined, the navvies found work building the railways. The word navvy described any labourer who worked on any large-scale civil engineering project undertaken in Victorian Britain.

Edwin Chadwick reported on the atrocious working conditions existing at many railway building sites; the navvies lived in huts they had erected themselves and sometimes meant fourteen or fifteen men lodged together. Their job was dangerous and they were prone to both fatal accidents and severe injury. When a navvy died his family was never compensated by the company or the contractor. The *tommy shops* on site and provided by the contractor charged exorbitant prices for everything. Wages were only paid at irregular intervals and Chadwick argued that the introduction of regulations could stop the atrocities.

A Select Committee on Railway Labourers was convened. Evidence was taken first from a surgeon on the Sheffield to Manchester line who stated that no contractor made enquiries when men's limbs were blown off and no provision was made by the company for accommodation of the sick. This was a common occurrence around the country. The select committee also took evidence from a few navvies who stated that amongst them were many men who saved their money rather than spending it all on drink; they suggested that if paid more frequently, the men would consider working for less; the main issue amongst them was the insecurity of employment.

Navvies were found in all areas of the country and although many travelled with their employers to work on projects across Britain, the contractors also recruited men locally from areas close to the construction site. It is often thought that most navvies were Irish, but although large numbers of Irish men travelled to Britain to become navvies, they were a minority amongst the thousands of men involved in the construction of the railways.

Navvying demanded strength and physical stamina. A large number of navvies had previously worked as agricultural labourers and as such were accustomed to hard and sometimes tiring work. However, it took up to a year to train a labourer as a navvy who frequently shifted over twenty tons of earth in a day. Some children less than ten years old often worked as navvies alongside their fathers or older brothers, and some men worked into their sixties and seventies so lighter duties were available.

Maintaining an even gradient was important for any railway line. Excavation of cuttings and formation of embankments were therefore needed on a regular basis to overcome natural undulations in the countryside. Moving millions of tons of rock and soil from one place to another required thousands of navvies working with a pick, shovel and wheelbarrow. By the 1890s, steam-powered machinery was used but much of the work was still done manually. The steam excavators speeded up the excavation work but men had to follow close behind to shore up the steep and dangerous slopes created by the machines.

Men were also needed in the construction of tunnels, bridges and viaducts. The men who built these feats of engineering were also considered navvies although they were actually skilled workmen including blacksmiths, stonemasons, bricklayers, miners, engine drivers, carpenters, steel erectors and riveters. In addition, rock blasting, spoil tipping, ballasting and track-laying were also routine tasks that were part of a navvy's work.

Railway construction remained a dangerous occupation and accidents were considered an accepted risk especially for those building tunnels or using explosives for blasting. Most navvies had a long working day with some men working during the night. Initially the contractors had little thought for the well-being of the navvies and men were often poorly trained and inadequately supervised. Speed as opposed to safety, was the primary concern of the contractors as there was a need to complete their contracts on time. It was thought that navvies in the early years of railway construction were at a greater risk of injury and death than a soldier on the battlefield.

The construction of railway lines was very labour intensive and at its height one in every hundred working people was a navvy. At the height of railway building there were 250,000 navvies throughout the country. Fatalities were commonplace often caused by working on inclines where people were either thrown from bogies or even just walking and being run over by railway trucks. Reports of coroners' inquests in provincial newspapers are very revealing and often damning of the circumstances of "accidental deaths". Coroners and their jurors travelled to the railway to view the bodies of men killed in accidents, and in some locations a dead house (mortuary) was provided to house the corpses. Men were often transported by horse and cart a number of miles away to hospitals when they were injured; some of them did not survive. Local graveyards can tell stories of deaths within railway navvy communities. Unmarked navvy graves also exist in most areas sometimes because actual names were never established.

Disease and epidemics were commonplace within communities including smallpox, known to have been the case at Ribblehead on the Settle to Carlisle railway and even murders took place, often in local hostelries. There were also fights between the navvies resulting in injuries which sometimes left navvies unable to work.

# GLOSSARY OF MEDICAL TERMS

| | |
|---|---|
| **boluses or pills** | boluses weigh more than six grains: pills weigh less than six grains |
| **blistering or vesiculation** | to raise a blister on the skin to correct inflammation, fevers, gout, hysteria |
| **calomel** | white powder of mercurious chloride used as a purgative |
| **cataplasm** | see poultice |
| **cyclophosphamide** | the active element in nitrogen mustard (mustard gas) |
| **collyrium (collyria)** | archaic term for a lotion or liquid eyewash |
| **consumption** | see phthisis |
| **corrody** | a lifetime allowance of food, clothing, shelter and care from an abbey or monastery |
| **dermal (cutaneous)** | to do with the skin or *dermis* |
| **diphtheria** | known as the *kissing disease;* common childhood infectious |
| **erethism** | commonly known as *mad hatter's disease;* a neurological disorder derived from mercury poisoning |
| **edema or oedema** | also known as dropsy; the build-up of fluid in the body's tissue |
| **foxglove (digitalis)** | commonly used in treatment of dropsy |
| **fomentations** | warm medicated lotions used for relief |
| **fistular cavity** | surgical passage between a hollow or tubular organ and the body surface |
| **laudanum** | tincture of opium diluted in alcohol) known as the *aspirin of the nineteenth century.* Reddish-brown in colour and extremely bitter, laudanum contains several opium alkaloids, including morphine and codeine and historically used to treat a variety of conditions, but its principal use was as a pain medication and cough suppressant. |
| **methane** | also known as firedamp; an explosive gas mixture found in mines |

| | |
|---|---|
| mithridate (*mithridatium*) | a semi-mythical remedy with as many as sixty-five ingredients, used as an antidote for poisoning |
| mustard gas | chemical weapon used extensively in WWI; see cyclophosphamide |
| Paris green | pigment in Victorian wallpaper and contained arsenic |
| phossy jaw | known as *phosphorus necrosis* of the jaw; an occupational disease of matchmakers |
| poliomyelitis | infectious disease primarily affecting children; invades the nervous system by infecting the spinal cord then the brain which resulted in limb paralysis |
| poultice or cataplasm | soft moist material, warmed and pressed to the body to relieve inflammation |
| phrenology | study of the shape/size of the cranium; supposed to indicate character and mental abilities |
| phthisis | pulmonary tuberculosis, a progressive wasting disease |
| pulmonary siderosis | see siderosis. Also known as *Welder's disease* |
| scarlet fever | known as *scarlatina*; bacterial infection mainly affecting children |
| silicosis | lung fibrosis, caused by inhaling silica dust |
| siderosis | similar to silicosis but caused by metallic dust; sometimes known as *grinder's rot* |
| sexually-transmitted disease | bacterial disease infecting the genitals |
| stramonium | a herbal medicine which caused hallucinations |
| syphilis | also referred to as the French pox, a sexually-transmitted disease |
| tolu balsam | used in medicines and as a flavouring agent in foods; originates from Columbia and Peru |
| typhoid | known as enteric fever; infectious bacterial fever displaying red spots and severe intestinal problems |
| Venice treacle | known medically as *theriac* or *theriaca*, an antidote remedy for poison |
| vesiculation | see blistering |
| whooping cough | medically known as *pertussis*; an intensive cough, especially infecting children. |

# BIBLIOGRAPHY AND SOURCES

## Bibliography

Bronstein, Jamie, L., *Caught in the Machinery – Workplace Accidents and Injured Workers in Nineteenth-Century Britain* (Stanford University Press 2007)

Hatcher, John *The Black Death: The Intimate Story of a Village in Crisis 1345–1350* (Weidenfield & Nicolson 2008)

Hutchinson, Iain, *A History of Disability in Nineteenth-Century Scotland* (Edwin Mellen Press 2007)

Lee, W R., *Emergence of Occupational Medicine in Victorian Times* (British Journal of Industrial Medicine Vol 30 1973)

Reinhardt, C., *A Handbook of The Open-air Treatment and Life in an Open-air Sanatorium* (John Bale 1902)

Williams, John, L., *Accidents and Ill Health at Work (Staples 1960)*

## Sources

British Medical Journal No 2630 *Quacks and Quackery* 1911

The Wellcome Collection *Causes of Accidental Death in Victorian Britain. The Financial Times*

Robinson, J, *Exposition of Hair Powder Acts (Paternoster Row 1795)*

University of London 1984 Audio-Visual Centre. *The Evolution of Community Medicine.* The first of a short series of lectures by Sidney Chave on the rise of the Public Health Movement.

# FURTHER READING

Bartrip, P., and Fenn, P.T., *The Measurement of Safety: Factory Accident Statistics in Victorian and Edwardian Britain.* (Historical Research 2007)

Freer, Wendy, *Women and Children of the Cut* (Railway and Canal Historical Society 1995)

Lawrence, Christopher, *Medicine in the Making of Modern Britain 1700-1920* (Routledge 1994)

Porter, Roy, *Quacks: Fakers and Charletons in English Medicine* (Tempus 2000)

# USEFUL WEBSITES

The British Newspaper Archive blog Occupations, nineteenth-century coal miners: blog.britishnewspaperarchive.co.uk/2017/08/30/occupations-19th-century-coal-miners/

The Railway Work, Life and Death project: www.railwayaccidents.port.ac.uk/

Working to Death in Victorian London (Nineteenth Century Working Class Life): www.youtube.com/watch?v=gpy_XdyDUdk

Victorian Web – Life in the Time of Cholera: How the Victorians Dealt with Epidemics: https://victorianweb.org/science/health/cholera/wenham.html

The Coalmining History Resource Centre – Coal Mining Accidents and Deaths Index 1700-2000: https://www.cmhrc.co.uk/site/disasters/index.html

Working to death in Victorian London https://www.youtube.com/watch?v=gpy_XdyDUdk

Life in the Time of Cholera: How the Victorians Dealt with Epidemics https://victorianweb.org/science/health/cholera/wenham.html

# USEFUL GUIDE TO THE CONTENTS
# OF ALL VOLUMES IN THE SERIES

Due to the comprehensive nature of this series, aspects of some topics inevitably appear in more than one volume. Therefore, in place of a long complicated index, this useful guide details the contents of each volume, including the appendices. The timeline is the same for every volume.

## VOLUME 1 – Medical Practices, Professions and Pioneers

Timeline
Introduction
Chapter 1     Evolving Medicine over the Centuries
Chapter 2     The Civilian Medical Profession
Chapter 3     The Hospital System
Chapter 4     Medical Advances and Pioneers
Conclusion

Appendices

1. Early medical training dates and establishments
2. Discovery of drugs in the nineteenth century
3. Dentistry timeline
4. Nightingale training school records
5. Miscellaneous nursing records
6. Training ships and the River Ambulance Service

List of illustrations
Glossary of medical terms relevant to the volume
Bibliography
Useful websites

## VOLUME 2 – Diseases, Remedies, Epidemics and Accidents

## VOLUME 3 – Births, Deaths, Funerals and Mental Illness

## VOLUME 4 – Military Medical Care